MODERN LEGAL STUDIES

DEVELOPMENT CONTROL

AUSTRALIA
The Law Book Company Ltd.
Sydney : Melbourne : Brisbane

CANADA AND U.S.A.
The Carswell Company Ltd.
Agincourt, Ontario

INDIA
N. M. Tripathi Private Ltd.
Bombay
and
Eastern Law House Private Ltd.
Calcutta
M.P.P. House
Bangalore

ISRAEL
Steimatzky's Agency Ltd.
Jerusalem : Tel Aviv : Haifa

MALAYSIA : SINGAPORE : BRUNEI
Malayan Law Journal (Pte.) Ltd.
Singapore

NEW ZEALAND
Sweet & Maxwell (N.Z.) Ltd.
Auckland

PAKISTAN
Pakistan Law House
Karachi

MODERN LEGAL STUDIES

DEVELOPMENT CONTROL

by
JOHN ALDER LL.B., B.C.L.
Lecturer in Law
University of Exeter

LONDON
SWEET & MAXWELL
1979

219117|000

Published in 1979 by
Sweet & Maxwell Limited of
11 New Fetter Lane, London
Computerset by
MFK Graphic Systems (Typesetting) Limited
Saffron Walden, Essex
Printed in Great Britain by
Page Bros (Norwich) Ltd

ISBN Hardback 0 421 25160 3
Paperback 0 421 25170 0

PREFACE

This small book was written with two main kinds of reader in mind. It is intended firstly for students of town and country planning law, both those reading for law degrees and those studying for town and country planning and estate management qualifications.

Secondly, it is intended for students of administrative law, a subject which undergraduates often complain is taught upon too abstract a level. The general principles of administrative law are considerably affected by the statutory context in which specific governmental powers are exercised. Development control provides an excellent example of such a context because it happens to raise many of the controversial problems which bedevil or intrigue administrative lawyers. These include in particular the question of *locus standi*; of estoppel, of the relationship between judicial review and statutory remedies, and the fundamental issue of the role of the courts in relation to discretionary powers. Development control powers also illustrate the structural weaknesses in the present system of local government. I have tried to emphasise these themes.

I have also tried to emphasise topics which are not dealt with in detail in the existing students' literature, in particular the important subject of planning agreements to which I have devoted a separate chapter.

I have concentrated upon law in the strict sense of the rules applied by the Superior Courts. These days when the term "black letter law" is used pejoratively, this needs an explanation if not an apology. I am aware that there are several different kinds of norm operating in the field of land use control including principles laid down by the Secretary of State, rules derived from planning practice and standards created by the Local Commissioners for Administration. Without venturing into jurisprudential debate as to the meaning of law, it is plausible to assert that the rules laid down by the ordinary courts are specially worthy of study, not only because they are chief in the hierarchy of norms governing public authorities but also because the ordinary courts provide the only genuinely independent machinery for settling disputes between citizen and official, this being what administrative law is all about.

I have not therefore attempted a full description of how planning works but I have tried to identify problems and also to draw attention to areas where the assumptions of the planners seem to be at variance with the views of the Courts. Where appropriate, I have made some comparisons with United States law.

I owe grateful thanks to the following people: to my wife who helped to prepare the tables; to Professor Patrick McAuslan, the General Editor of this series, Vivienne Gay of Exeter University and Colin Munro of Durham University, each of whom read and commented upon individual chapters; to Jane Edworthy, Nancy Scattergood and Rosemary Sookias who typed and retyped the manuscript; and last but not least to the final year Planning Law students of Exeter University who stimulated me into thinking about the subject more than I might otherwise have done. Of these, Sara Coate and Susie Wilson saved me from some culpable errors.

The law is stated from sources available on May 1, 1979.

May 1979   JOHN ALDER
                                    University of Exeter

CONTENTS

OTHER BOOKS IN THE SERIES

TABLE OF CASES

TABLE OF STATUTES

xviii

Table of Statutes

TABLE OF RULES

RULES OF THE SUPREME COURT

ABBREVIATIONS

Cullingworth – *Town and Country Planning in Britain*. J. B. Cullingworth (6th ed. 1976)

De Smith – *Judicial Review of Administrative Action*. S. A. de Smith (3rd ed. 1973)

Dobry – *Review of the Development Control System* (HMSO 1975), George Dobry, Q.C.

Encyclopaedia – *Encyclopaedia of Planning Law and Practice*. 4 volumes

Hamilton – *Development and Planning*. R. N. D. Hamilton (6th ed. 1975)

Heap – *An Outline of Planning Law*. Sir Desmond Heap (7th ed. 1978)

J.P.L. – *Journal of Planning and Environment Law*

McAuslan – *Land, Law and Planning*. Patrick McAuslan (1975)

Purdue – *Cases and Materials on Planning Law*. Michael Purdue (1977)

Telling – *Planning Law and Procedure*. A. E. Telling (5th ed. 1977)

Wade – *Administrative Law*. H. W. R. Wade (4th ed. 1977)

Wraith and Lamb – *Public Inquiries as an Instrument of Government*. R. E. Wraith and G. B. Lamb (1971)

Chapter 1

GENERAL BACKGROUND

The Nature of Development Control

Few people would deny that in this crowded island it is proper for Government to impose restrictions upon the way land is used. What is controversial is the form such restrictions should take and the extent to which the ordinary citizen should have a say in the matter. Since 1947 there has been in force a system of town and country planning which is probably the most comprehensive and sophisticated in the world. The Town and Country Planning Act 1947 conferred wide discretionary powers upon local and central government to prohibit undesirable uses of land by private landowners, and more restricted powers to take positive steps to insure that land is used for projects which are thought desirable in the public interest. It is with one aspect of town and country planning law that this book is concerned. The 1947 Act has been repealed but its general principles survive in the form of the Town and Country Planning Act 1971, a consolidating Act, which has itself been amended (hereinafter called the Act).[1]

Development control is essentially a method of licensing. It derives from section 23 (1) of the Act which provides that "Planning permission is required for the carrying out of any development of land." Applications for planning permission are made to a local authority and there is a right of appeal to the Secretary of State for the Environment. The application and ramifications of this principle together with its qualifications and enforcement machinery will form the subject-matter of later chapters. This preliminary chapter will discuss the general background to the development control system and introduce some pervasive problems. It must be emphasised now that the term "development" which defines the extent of the licensing power has a very wide meaning (see Chap. 2). It embraces most substantial changes, either physically to the land itself, or in the activities carried out upon it. Thus the private householder who takes in paying guests may be "developing" as much as is the property speculator who builds a housing estate on green fields. The width of the term is in itself a source of difficulty since, while it gives considerable scope for the activities of planning authorities, it does at the same time create the risk that trivial or irrelevant matters occupy the time of the zealous official. Development control is a fertile field for accusations upon the theme of bureaucratic red tape, and delay in the processing of applications is a subject of considerable concern. Nevertheless the lawyer is concerned with procedural safeguards such as the right to a hearing which must inevitably cause delay, as the price to be paid if justice is to be seen to be done (see Chap. 8).

Development control is worth studying for several reasons. It is the part of planning law which most affects the ordinary citizen and is thus of particular interest to the lawyer, both as a conveyancer and the champion of individual liberties. It is one of the most intensively litigated areas of administrative law and provides a focus for the analysis of several difficult and controversial questions in the field of judicial review of administrative action. These include estoppel, *locus standi*, the application of the rules of natural justice, and the distinction between fact and policy. Development control raises the general question of the extent to which the courts are able and willing to interfere with the discretionary powers of public authorities. It is a prominent characteristic of the Act that it confers wide discretions upon planning authorities not only as to policy but also to determine the existence of facts (*e.g.* p. 140, below).

The carrying-out of development without permission is not in itself a criminal offence. Nor, although there is no direct authority on the point (*cf. Buxton* v. *Minister of Housing* [1961] 1 Q.B. 278), can it be a civil wrong actionable at the suit of a private person. Section 23 (1) imposes an obligation to obtain planning permission and to that extent development without permission is unlawful. The duty however is a public one and is not owed to a class of persons sufficiently specific to allow them to sue in tort (see *Winfield and Jolowicz on Tort* (10th ed.), pp. 128–130).

The role of the individual in the planning process involves both attempts to challenge decisions taken by the planning authority, and the claim that members of the public are entitled to "participate" in the decision-making process. "Participation" in this context is rather a misnomer since the demand is merely that the public be able to express their views to the authority on a specific proposal, not that there should be machinery, such as referenda, for public decision-making. Apart from considerations of delay the notion of public participation has been criticised as militating against the principle of representative democracy, and of being futile since "participations" are often based on ignorance and self-interest (see Heap, *The Land and the Development* (Hamlyn Lectures (1976), pp. 35–41). It is also alleged to be socially divisive since the wealthy and leisured often make the most effective "participants" and concern for the environment is entirely consistent with the preservation of property values, but not always with improving the living standards of the poor.[2]

Enforcement is at the discretion of the local planning authority which is empowered, but not obliged, to serve an enforcement notice upon the offending landowner and certain other persons (section 87). The notice requires the unauthorised development to cease and steps to be taken to restore the land to its original condition. Disobedience is a criminal offence punishable by fine, and the authority may in some cases enter the land and put matters right themselves. Enforcement notices are a fruitful source of litigation since their service and implementation are fraught with procedural pitfalls and there is elaborate machinery for challenging them. The chance to contest an enforcement notice furnishes the recalcitrant developer with a valuable opportunity to buy time (see Chap. 7).

It has also been held that unauthorised development can be restrained by means of an injunction. This can be sought by the Attorney-General, as the Crown officer responsible for enforcing the law, either on his own motion, or in relator proceedings where he lends his name to an action brought by someone else (*Att.-Gen.* v. *Bastow* [1957] 1 Q.B. 514, *Att.-Gen.* v. *Smith* [1958] 2 Q.B. 173). A private person could cure his own lack of standing by requesting the Attorney-General's aid but the Attorney has a discretion whether or not to intervene which is apparently not reviewable by the court (see *Gouriet* v. *N.U.P.O.W.* [1978] A.C. 435). Apart from this procedure a private individual could not apply for an injunction since the remedy lies only in favour of a person whose legal rights are infringed (*Gouriet* case, above). It has been held however that a local authority, thanks to the wording of section 222 (1) of the Local Government Act 1972 can apply for an injunction to protect public right in its own name and does not need to invoke the aid of the Attorney-General. This provides that "where a local authority considers it expedient for the promotion or protection of the interests of the inhabitants of their area ... they may ... in the case of civil proceedings institute them in their own name" (see *Solihull B.C.* v. *Maxfern Ltd*. [1977] 1 W.L.R. 127, *Stafford B.C.* v. *Elkenford Ltd*. [1977] 1 W.L.R. 324, *Kent C.C.* v. *Batchelor* (1976) 33 P. & C.R. 185).

The possibility of obtaining an injunction raises several difficulties concerning the relationship between the injunction and the statutory enforcement procedure (see p. 158, below). It suffices to say here that the availability of the injunction raises a constitutional issue, in that a combination of executive and court can effectively increase the statutory penalty for disobeying an enforcement notice. The penalty for defying an injunction can be unlimited imprisonment for contempt of court whereas a fine is the punishment provided by statute. By specifying a modest penalty Parliament has expressed the social value which it places upon compliance with planning law. Should a court be able to issue another remedy which represents a different estimate of the severity of the offence? In *Kent C.C.* v. *Batchelor* (above) Talbot J. justified the use of the injunction by emphasising that the Act was designed to protect the public interest in natural beauty as well as to create criminal liability and therefore a preventative remedy was appropriate. This is a distinction without substance. The creation of a criminal offence is merely the procedural means chosen by Parliament to protect the public interest in natural beauty. In the nature of things no legal remedy is literally preventative. Injunctions and criminal penalties are alike intended to deter. The sanction can be applied only after the offence is committed or the injunction disobeyed. The difference between them as deterrents lies only in the severity of the punishment.

There is in general no right to compensation in respect of planning restrictions.[3] Before 1947 there existed a limited system of planning control which depended upon a "planning scheme." This zoned land for particular categories of development, and compensation was sometimes payable. It is believed that the obligation to pay compensation frustrated the aims of the legislation. The prospect of having to spend money discouraged local authorities from any radical exercise of their powers and where planning schemes were made at all, they tended either merely to reflect the status quo or to be extravagantly generous in permitting development. Thus in 1937 enough land was provisionally allocated for housing to provide for a population of nearly 300 million (see Royal Commission on the Distribution of the Industrial Population, Cmnd. 6153 (1940), pp. 112–126. 1977 population of the United Kingdom was 54 million).

The courts have held that the presumption of statutory interpretation against interference with property rights without compensation does not generally apply to governmental restrictions upon the use of land, as opposed to confiscation of the land itself (but see below). The right freely to use land cannot since 1947 be regarded as an incident of ownership: *Westminster Bank Ltd.* v. *Minister of Housing and Local Government* [1970] 2 W.L.R. 645, 652. (But compare *Hall & Co.* v. *Shoreham U.D.C.* [1964] 1 W.L.R. 240 where the authority's interference was tantamount to confiscation. See also *France, Fenwick & Co.* v. *R.* [1927] 1 K.B. 458 and *Belfast Corporation* v. *O.D. Cars Ltd.* [1960] A.C. 490.)

The same view has been taken by the United States Supreme Court in cases where the constitutionality of land use restrictions has been challenged. It has been held that it is necessary for the public welfare for government to impose restrictions upon the use of land. Such restrictions do not constitute a confiscation of land so as to require payment of compensation under the constitution unless they are so drastic as to deprive the landowner of any economic return from his land. (See *Village of Euclid* v. *Amber Realty* Cr. 272 U.S. 365 (1926), *Nectow* v. *City of Cambridge* 277 U.S. 183 (1928),

Pennsylvania Coal Co. v. *Mahon* 260 U.S. 393 (1922).)

The question of compensation leads to a correlative issue. The grant of planning permission will, if economic circumstances are favourable to development, lead to a great increase in the value of the land in question (*cf. Camrose* v. *Basingstoke Corporation* [1966] 1 W.L.R. 1100). What should happen to this profit, known as development value or betterment and contrasted in planning jargon with "existing" or "current" use value? This question has never been satisfactorily answered and is politically controversial. A logical and doctrinaire application of the principle that ownership does not carry development rights (which is expressed by the absence of compensation) would dictate that all development value should be appropriated by the state. This principle was indeed adopted by the Parliament which enacted the original 1947 scheme. This provided that a development charge be paid to a public authority by those who realised the fruits of planning permission, normally on a sale of land.

Such a concept is prey not only to clashes of political ideology but also to practical and economic difficulties. The original scheme was abandoned in 1954, partly because of political pressures and partly because it was alleged to have an adverse effect upon the supply of land available for development, and to inflate land prices. Vendors were accused of adding on the development charge to what would otherwise have been the market price (*cf. Earl Fitzwilliam's Wentworth Estates* v. *Minister of Housing and Local Government* [1952] A.C. 362).

Since then the treatment of development value has fluctuated according to the political complexion of the government in office (see Cullingworth, Chap. 7).[4] However there exists a broad measure of agreement that a landowner is not entitled to keep the whole development value of his land since it is unearned profit made possible by government action. At present a development land tax is payable under the

Development Land Tax Act 1976. This can be up to 80 per cent. of the development value of the land payable either upon an actual disposal when the development value is realised, or upon a "deemed disposal" where the land is not sold or leased but the owner commences work on his development, such as laying the foundations (see D.L.T.A. 1976, Sched. 1, Pt. I). The details of the tax are outside the scope of this book, but in any event it is designed only as a temporary measure. The Community Land Act 1975 constitutes a further attempt to transfer development value to the community and is of more general significance. This Act requires that, subject to some exemptions, land suitable for development be acquired by a local authority at a price which ignores development value. The authority will either develop the land itself or transfer it at full market price back to the private sector, thus creaming off development value for the public benefit, as well as ensuring that the Government has positive influence over development. Whether the life of this Act will be any longer than that of its predecessors is problematical.

However the Community Land Act has been opposed less strenuously than might be expected in the light of the opposition to the White Paper which introduced it (Land, Cmnd. 5730 (1974); see Cullingworth, pp. 144–146). This may be partly because it has been utilised only on a small scale. The Act is essentially enabling and ministerial orders subject to Parliamentary approval are required to bring its various provisions into effect. This will be done in stages. At present the Act empowers but does not oblige local authorities to acquire land for development. There is no indication that an order imposing a general duty to acquire land will be made in the foreseeable future. Another reason for the muted opposition to the Act may be a desire to achieve certainty in the matter of development value.

Moreover, the Secretary of State has exercised his powers

under the Act to exclude a wide range of small private development from the powers of compulsory acquisition (Community Land (Excepted Development) Regulations 1976, No. 331). The Act is far from the monster of land nationalisation that opponents of the Bill envisaged. (See *The Times*, [1976] February 19, April 5, April 6, November 16; [1977] June 10).

The theoretical possibility has been presented of achieving justice by transferring some of the profits made by the person granted planning permission to the landowner who is refused permission. This is based upon the assumption that development value, like energy is never created anew but shifts from one piece of land to another so that A's gain is B's loss. Such a principle appears to be unworkable because there is no direct correspondence between development value and the amount of money required for compensation. Development value can only be confiscated when actually realised by a sale of the land. Moreover, because of the vagaries of human behaviour it is reasonably certain that less land will actually be developed than could in theory be developed. Development value is therefore said to be "floating" value. Thus, if 10,000 acres are capable of development for housing, perhaps houses will actually be built on half that much. Nevertheless if the 10,000 acres is refused permission for development each landowner can equally claim that the floating value could settle on his land. The position is like that of a lottery. Thus the total compensation bill, adding together each separate claim, will always exceed the money actually available when development takes place.

It was this consideration which *inter alia* persuaded the promoters of the 1947 Act to abandon a general right to compensation (see Report of the Uthwatt Committee on Compensation and Betterment, Cmnd. 6386 (1942)).

This, in brief outline, is the mechanics of the development control system. We can now consider it in relation to other aspects of planning law.

Planning powers can be broadly classified into positive and negative powers. A positive power is intended to ensure that land is used in a specific way. The positive power *par excellence* is therefore the compulsory purchase order. Negative powers, among which the development control machinery is pre-eminent, merely forbid undesirable activities but leave the initiative to propose and carry out development with the landowner. It is often said that the British planning system is inadequately endowed with positive powers. The Community Land Act 1975 with its wide compulsory purchase powers is capable of remedying this. The Act is intended not only to deal with the problem of land values, but also to achieve positive planning through the medium of public ownership of development land. The relationship between this Act and the general development control machinery will be discussed in Chapter 5. Various other statutes, for example housing and new Towns legislation, confer positive powers for specific purposes related to planning.

The Town and Country Planning Act 1971 contains limited powers of compulsory acquisition. These derive from section 112, which confers power on the Secretary of State to authorise local planning authorities to acquire land which in his opinion needs treatment as a whole, "by development, redevelopment or improvement" (or for certain ancillary purposes). Having acquired land the authority may, with the consent of the Secretary of State, transfer it to other persons subject to conditions as to how it is to be developed (section 123). This facilitates co-operative schemes involving for example the modernisation of town centres, between public authorities and private developers. Areas appropriate for this kind of comprehensive treatment will usually be designated in the authorities' development plan as "action areas" (see below, p. 15) but formal designation is not a condition precedent to the exercise of the power (see Franks Committee on Administrative Tribunals and Inquiries, Cmnd. 218 (1957), para. 380). The Act also authorises compulsory acquisition where the Secretary of State is satisfied "that it is expedient to acquire the land immediately for a purpose which it is necessary to achieve in the interests of the proper planning of an area in which the land is situated" (section 112 (1) (*d*)) [5.]

Another kind of positive power is provided by section 52. This allows planning authorities to enter into agreements with landowners for the purpose of restricting and regulating the use of their land. These agreements can be used as a means of positive planning. Thus a landowner may promise to provide land for public amenities. Problems arise out of the relationship between such agreements and the general development control powers, and concern particularly the legality of "bargaining" for planning permission (see Chap. 6 below). This is an area where the suspicion of official corruption is particularly prevalent.

When granting planning permission an authority may attach "such conditions as they think fit" (section 29 (1)). These can also be used to achieve positive purposes, by requiring for example the provision of community facilities on the development land.

Planning Policies—Development Plans

A local planning authority is obliged to carry out periodic surveys of its territory and to produce a written development plan which sets outs it proposals for the use of land. Development control decisions are then taken in the light of the plan. The plan is confirmed by the Secretary of State, so that local, regional and national policies can be co-ordinated. Central government involvement in the planning process is a

B

fundamental characteristic of the legislation because in a small and densely populated country local government boundaries cannot define areas that are socially and economically self-contained.

Development plans are from the legal point of view relatively unimportant. Decisions in individual cases do not have to conform to them. The Act merely requires that the provisions of the development plan be taken into account along with other relevant considerations. Discretion in individual cases is the hall-mark of the development control system (for specific legal consequences of development plans see Telling, p. 76).

Whether a development plan is a useful guide to decision-making depends upon three main factors; first the amount of detail in it; secondly the relationship between those who make the plan and those who make development control decisions; and thirdly the draftsman's ability to foresee the future. In all these aspects, although there have been major changes in the law since 1947, the position is still unsatisfactory. Perhaps this is inevitable since "planning," if it is intended to embrace wide social and economic considerations, presupposes an ability to foretell the future that is beyond the range of existing social science techniques.

Under the 1947 Act a development plan consisted of a written statement of objectives and a map. Its most important characteristic was that it allocated land to specific uses (residential, agricultural, industrial etc.) and also defined the sites of proposed public works. The Act did not specify the amount of detail required but regulations prescribed the scale of the maps. Supplementary plans could be made dealing in greater detail with what were called comprehensive development areas and regulations governing these required consider-able detail including the intensity with which land and buildings were to be occupied, or the permissible amount of floor space. Similarly a supplementary town map could be produced specifying proposals for complex areas such as town centres. These plans, even the most detailed, left room for considerable discretion in individual cases. Thus, where floor space was prescribed, the precise distribution of the allocation (*e.g.* the choice between five floors of 10,000 square feet, or 10 floors of 5,000 square feet) would be left to the discretion of the development control official.

This system attracted considerable criticism and by the Town and Country Planning Act 1968 was replaced with a fundamentally different sort of development plan (under transitional arrangements (see 1971 Act, Scheds. 5 and 7) the old style plans remain in force until the new plan becomes effective).

Local planning authorities are obliged by section 6 of the Act to prepare and submit new style plans for confirmation by the Secretary of State. There is no time limit for the fulfilment of this obligation and readers will not be surprised to learn that despite a target date of 1979 only a minority of authorities have submitted their plans.

The criticisms of old style plans were two-fold, but essentially concerned the amount of detail in them (see Report of the Planning Advisory Group, *The Future of Development Plans* (1965) and White Paper on Town and Country Planning, Cmnd. 3333, (1967) (31 M.L.R. 55)).

First, the process of plan-making and confirmation was extremely lengthy; the Minister was obliged to hold an inquiry into all objections, and confirmation of plans often took three years and sometimes considerably longer. The plan identified specific pieces of land and thus directly affected property values. Objections could be numerous and based not on policy matters but on special pleading in defence of vested interests. Inquiries were normally conducted in a quasi-judicial manner, and in accordance with traditional practice the procedure was modelled broadly on that of a court of law, *i.e.* in a manner geared to the defence of rights and the analysis of detailed facts, but not to the discussion of policy.

Secondly, the content of the plan fell between two stools. It was not sufficiently detailed to provide a precise guide to the citizen as to how decisions were likely to be made, but at the same time the requirement of a map made it rigid and inflexible and liable to become obsolete when changes took place in matters outside the authority's control, for example, the closure of a factory, or a new road project.

Because the emphasis was on the allocation of land to specific uses it was difficult to express in the plan matters which transcended the local authority's geographical boundaries. For example, one urban authority might plan on the assumption that its surplus population would be accommodated by neighbouring rural authorities. Plans produced by its neighbours would not necessarily take this factor into account. This problem is, of course, inherent in the English system of theoretically autonomous local government units but was accentuated by the old form of development plan. The Minister has power to integrate the activities of neighbouring authorities, either through the confirmation machinery or specifically by setting up joint planning boards (section 1 (2)) but this is rarely exercised. Local government autonomy, or the appearance thereof, is a relevant political consideration.

Other factors which the old-style development plan could ignore would be general matters outside the direct control of the authority such as the traffic needs of the area and the balance between public and private transport.

Even the more detailed comprehensive development area plans were unsatisfactory in that, because of the threat of compulsory purchase, such designation "blighted" the land, and landowners were discouraged from maintaining or improving their properties.[6]

In practice those responsible for development control

decisions often make their own unofficial maps drawn to any scale they like. These "bottom drawer" plans are free from statutory regulations and can be taken into account without necessarily being disclosed to the public. This avoids blight but is not conducive either to predictability, or democracy.

The 1968 Act adopted the device, now contained in Part II of the 1971 Act, of prescribing two kinds of development plan, one called a structure plan which outlines general policy and the other, a local plan, which makes detailed proposals within the area covered by the structure plan.

Structure plans have to be prepared by county councils and confirmed by the Secretary of State. They differ in major respects from old-style plans. First there is no land use allocation map. The plan consists of a written statement of generalised objectives. This is intended to lessen delay at the confirmation stage by removing matters of detail from the province of the Secretary of State and thereby reducing the number of objections to the plan. Secondly, the Act expressly requires a wide range of factors to be considered, including the social and economic characteristics of its area, transport, and the distribution of population (section 6). The authority is obliged to consider these factors in relation to neighbouring areas which affect its own (section 6 (3)), and to state the relationship of its policies to those of its neighbours. One of the tasks of the structure plan is to translate national and regional planning policies into local terms. Moreover, under the Town and Country Planning (Amendment) Act 1972 local authorities can combine together to produce joint structure plans (section 10 of the 1971 Act).

The structure plan does not descend to prescribing specific uses for any given piece of land. There is however one exception. This is the case of "action areas," which are areas intended for comprehensive treatment, and the successors of the old C.D.A.s. These have to be indicated in the plan (section

7 (5)). However, as there is no map the boundaries of the area will be left unclear. It is intended thereby to lessen the risk of blight. While it is true that blight may be less serious the uncertainty as to what land is affected is likely to mean that the blight will be spread, albeit more thinly, over a wider area.

The generalised nature of structure plans may speed up the plan-making process. The plan will also be less likely to become obsolete because of specific unforeseeable changes. However, there are two obvious weaknesses.

First, the lack of a map makes it an even more uncertain guide to development control decisions than the older system. Experience with the first plans produced under the new arrangements and particularly with the Greater London Development Plan (see Roberts, *Reform of Planning Law*, Chap. 7) indicate that structure plan policy statements sometimes consist of idealistic and platitudinous propositions stated at a high level of generality and providing no guidance as to the choices to be made in dealing with specific problems. Thus a preliminary statement of objectives published by one county council includes the following: "the need to conserve agricultural land and the environment should be borne in mind at all times"; "to make the best use of existing infrastructure"; "to make the best use of natural resources of commercial value." Such statements not only have very little meaning but are also conflicting. Useful information can on the other hand be given where a structure plan designates geographical areas within the county where growth should be either encouraged or actively discouraged (see *e.g.* Devon Draft Structure Plan). Thus a plan may indicate areas where broadly defined types of development (*e.g.* industry, or housing) are likely to be favourably treated.[7]

Secondly, the obligation to consider such factors as population or economic trends imposes an impossible burden upon an authority since these matters depend upon future events beyond both the control and the foresight of any human being. Thus the lengthy process of carrying out a survey and formulating proposals may become merely an academic exercise and, even though periodic reviews of the plan are required, irrelevant to the day-to-day business of development control.

Local plans are more like the old-style development plans. They include both map and written statement and are intended to be a more detailed application of the policies outlined in the structure plan. They must conform "generally to the structure plan" (section 14 (2)). They can be based on any geographical area within the county or alternatively be specialised subject plans dealing, for example, with transport. There can be any number of local plans within a county, but there is no obligation to prepare local plans except for action areas, or in other cases where the Secretary of State so directs. The most important legal characteristic of local plans is that they do not require confirmation by the Secretary of State, but need only be adopted by the authority itself, which is thus judge in its own cause.

The Secretary of State can however call in any local plan for approval and copies of all local plans must be submitted to him prior to adoption (section 14 (3); see Heap, pp. 72–75).

The justification for dispensing with central government confirmation is the practical one of reducing delay. Local plans are concerned with matters of detail and Parliament wished to take the heavy burden of this work off the shoulders of central government. In theory the policies set out in the structure plan are intended to settle matters of principle so that the production of local plans should involve the relatively uncontroversial task of applying an already accepted principle to detailed circumstances. Local plans can however be prepared, but not adopted in advance of the structure plan, which, bearing in mind that responsibility for preparing structure and local plans is allocated to different authorities, is a further source of difficulty. Objections to local plans are more likely to be forthcoming than to the structure plan which does not directly threaten any specific piece of land.

It would be surprising if the production of two plans results in less delay than that produced by the old system, and the new system is unlikely to produce less "blight" than the old, at least in connection with areas covered by local plans.

More fundamentally there is a serious flaw in the institutional arrangements governing plan-making and its relationship with development control. When the 1968 Act introduced the new system the general question of local government reform was also under review. Changes in planning law were made on the assumption that both aspects of planning—development plans and control—should be in the charge of the same local authority (see Royal Commission on Local Government in England, Cmnd. 4040 (1966–69)). A change of government in 1970 invalidated this assumption and the Local Government Act 1972 divided planning functions between different authorities, thereby setting the stage for conflicts of interest. It must be borne in mind that in constitutional theory local government bodies do not form a hierarchy but are, subject to central government controls, autonomous authorities whose relationship is based upon a division of function.

Structure plans are made by the county councils whereas local plans and development control are primarily the responsibility of district councils. Not only is this arrangement conducive to conflict, but it raises practical difficulties since the smaller district councils may be unable to employ enough well-qualified staff to service their newly-established planning departments.[8]

There are complicated provisions in the 1972 Act dealing with possible conflicts between county and district. They add further procedural requirements to the decision-making process and therefore exacerbate delay.[9]

First, the county council must under section 10 C of the 1971 Act (inserted by L.G.A. 1972) prepare a "development plan scheme" which allocates the responsibility for making plans between the various authorities in its area and under which it could reserve the plan-making power to itself (as it also can by a provision to this effect in the structure plan). However, the onus of proof to justify removing plan-making power from a district is on the county and a dissatisfied district council can make representations to the Secretary of State.

Secondly, before a local plan can be adopted the county council must certify that it conforms generally to the provisions of the structure plan, disputes being resolved by the Secretary of State (L.G.A. 1972, Sched. 16).

Machinery is also available to deal with conflicts between the development plan and development control decisions. This too introduces procedural complexities and uncertainties.

Certain types of application for planning permission are designated as "county matters" (L.G.A. 1972, Sched. 16, paras. 15 and 32). These include applications relating to mineral workings and ancillary activities, developments which are likely to conflict with fundamental provisions of the development plan or with other policy statements made by the county, development partly inside or outside a national park and development which concerns a "prescribed" operation or use. It is for the Secretary of State to make regulations containing the prescription. None have been made (L.G.A. 1972, section 270 (1)). The district council is required to forward county matters to the county for decision. It is however expressly provided that a failure to do so does not affect the validity of a planning permission (*ibid.*, para. 51 (1)). Moreover the question whether an application is "county" is decided by the district council and in the event of a dispute its decision would be overruled by the court or Secretary of State only if grossly unreasonable in the sense of being arbitrary and capricious (*Secretary of State for Education and Science* v. *Tameside M.B.C.* [1977] A.C. 1014). This is particularly important where the "county matter" is defined in nebulous terms.

To add to these difficulties, matters which are "county" because of conflict with the development plan or with county policy need be referred only if the district council proposes to grant permission. There may be cases where to refuse permission would be inconsistent with county policy, for example, where a district adopts the policy of discouraging development within an area designated for residential overspill by the county.

If the county proposes to grant permission in respect of a matter which is "county" because it departs from the development plan the proposal must be advertised and objections considered. The Secretary of State must in some cases be notified to give him a chance to "call in" the application for determination by himself (see Town and Country Planning (Development Plans) Direction 1975, Circular 96/75).

Finally, under L.G.A. 1972, Sched. 16, para. 19, a county planning authority may give directions to a district council as to how it is to determine an application "in any case where it appears to the county planning authority that any proposals in the application would substantially and adversely affect their interests as local planning authority." For reasons of political comity this wide and drastic power is unlikely much to be used. Where however a direction is given, a planning permission granted contrary to it would be *ultra vires*, there being no saving provision analogous to that relating to county matters.

Apart from the legal machinery numerous circulars have emanated from the Secretary of State recommending arrangements for co-operation between the local government units.

These are sometimes formulated as *development control schemes* (not to be confused with the statutory *development plan schemes*) which provide in detail for liaison between district and county. Such schemes sometimes define in considerable detail what kinds of application are to be regarded as county matters (see Cullingworth, pp. 116–120). Bearing in mind that local government reorganisation has roughly trebled the total number of planning authorities it is easy to agree with the writer who remarked of the new authorities that "they will be too busy co-ordinating and co-operating with each other to have much time and energy left to do any serious planning" and "there is a substantial risk that the complexities of the new system and the uncreative tensions which may well occur . . . will render wholly nugatory any improvements which the reforms of 1968 might have introduced into the new English system of planning" (Barendt (1974) 2 *Florida State University Law Review* 441).

Public Consultation

It is part of the conventional wisdom of planning that there should be an element of what it is fashionable to call "public participation" in the planning process. At the same time it is recognised that this is a cause of delay. One objective of the 1968 reforms of the development plan machinery was to provide an acceptable measure of public consultation (compare the position with respect to development *control* (pp. 81–85, below).

It has already been seen that the old-style development plan procedure entitled all objectors to be heard at an inquiry. The structure plan procedure which is contained in the 1971 Act as amended by the Town and Country Planning (Amendment) Act 1972 preserves the Secretary of State's obligation to consider all objections but gives no further right to be heard, thus abandoning the traditional and time-consuming public inquiry. Instead the legislation gives a broad discretion both to the local planning authority and to the Secretary of State as to the publicity to be given, to the choice of persons to be heard and the matters to be discussed. To compensate for this restriction upon the right to object, the Act introduces the principle that the public should be consulted at an early stage in the plan-making process, rather than, as under the old system, when the draft plan was completed and thus more difficult to contest. However the vague and generalised nature of structure plans is likely in itself to discourage objections and would certainly make the presentation of them more difficult. Lawyers are trained to argue about specific facts and defined claims and would not be at home at a structure plan inquiry.

The requirements as to public consultation are minimal as regards enforceable legal obligations, but open-ended in the sense that an authority is given the power to embark upon elaborate exercises in "participation" should it so desire. Central government publications including the report of the Skeffington Committee (*People and Planning* (D.O.E.) 1972) make suggestions as to how public opinion may be canvassed, and section 18 of the Act empowers the Secretary of State to make regulations governing, *inter alia*, the procedure for making and publicising structure plans. Regulations so far made have showed little official enthusiasm for "participation" and do not substantially amplify the statutory requirements (Town and Country Planning (Structure and Local Plans) Regulations) 1974 (No. 1486, P. III).

Section 8 governs publicity prior to the submission of the plan to the Secretary of State. Here the authority is obliged to take steps that *in its opinion* will ensure that adequate publicity is given to the report of the survey and to the matters which they propose to include in the plan. They must also give persons who "may be expected to desire an opportunity to make representations" an opportunity to do so, and must consider such representations.

These requirements, such as they are, must be complied with before the content of the plan is finally determined. The completed draft plan must be made available for public inspection and each copy must be accompanied by a statement of the time limit for making objections to the Secretary of State.

The obligation to consult the public at the formative stage of plan-making and therefore to introduce an element of "participation" is couched in subjective terms. Challenge in the courts to the adequacy of arrangements is therefore difficult. The applicant bears the heavy onus of showing that no reasonable man could regard the arrangements as providing "adequate publicity" (see *Rollo* v. *Minister of Town and Country Planning* [1948] 1 All E.R. 13, 17; *Thorneloe & Clarkson Ltd.* v. *Board of Trade* [1950] 2 All E.R. 245; *Agricultural etc. Training Board* v. *Aylesbury Mushrooms Ltd.* [1972] 1 W.L.R. 190). However it is unlikely that structure plans will be of enough concern to landowners to tempt them into litigation, and it is doubtful whether politically-motivated pressure groups would have sufficient *locus standi* (see *Buxton* v. *Minister of Housing* [1961], Q.B. 278, but *cf. Turner* v. *Secretary of State* (1973) 72 L.G.R. 380). There is no reported case where a development plan of any kind has been successfully challenged.

There is an internal control over the publicity arrangements in that when the local authority submits its plan to the Secretary of State it must inform him of the steps it has taken in respect of publicity. If on the basis of this he is dissatisfied he may refuse to confirm the plan and remit it with directions as to further steps to be taken. This sanction seems to be both weak and unrealistic.

The right to be heard has been abolished in relation to the Secretary of State's decision whether to confirm the plan. The

Secretary of State must consider all objections received in accordance with regulations, and he must also hold an "examination in public." Unlike the traditional public inquiry, no one has a right to be heard at it. The Secretary of State has a discretion to select both the participants and the matters to be discussed, the Act expressly providing that "the Secretary of State shall not be required to secure to any local planning authority or other person a right to be heard" (section 9 (5)). The examination in public is intended to be an informal discussion of important issues selected by the Secretary of State, and concerning in particular the relationship between the plan and central government policy. It is not an inquiry into objections. The Secretary of State can therefore, if he wishes, limit participants to persons having special knowledge relevant to the issues to be discussed. Representatives of interested public authorities are also likely to be invited to attend.

Unlike the traditional public inquiry the examination in public is not subject to the legal controls provided by the Tribunals and Inquiries Act 1971 except that it is supervised by the Council of Tribunals (Tribunals and Inquiries Act 1971, s. 1). Thus the Secretary of State does not have to give reasons for his decision whether or not to confirm the structure plan (*cf.* section 9 (8)). Similarly the procedural rules made under the Tribunals and Inquiries Act relating *inter alia* to the introduction of fresh evidence after the inquiry do not apply to development plan inquiries (see S.I. 1974 No. 419). Thus there is a sharp distinction between these inquiries and those which have to be held in connection with development control appeal decisions (see Chap. 8). The latter partake far more of a quasi-judicial character and are subject to greater legal controls.

It is unlikely that the courts can exercise significant control over the examination in public except upon the basis of gross arbitrariness or unfairness. For example, a court could interfere if the Secretary of State selected only representatives of government departments to participate, or discussed a controversial issue and invited only supporters of one side to attend. However, the direct impact of structure plans upon the ordinary citizen is likely to be so small that there may be few private persons motivated to attend the examination in public, and even fewer moved to litigate.[10]

In the case of local plans similar provision is made by section 12 for public consultation at the formative stage, but the procedure prior to adoption is different. A hearing or public inquiry of the traditional type, before a person appointed by the Secretary of State, must be held, thus giving objectors a right to be heard (section 13 (1); see Town and Country Planning (Structure and Local Plans Regulations) 1974 (No. 1486), Pt. VII). In theory objections at this stage should concern only matters of detail because the confirmation of the structure plan will make questions of broad principle and policy *res judicatae*. Whether or not an individual objector, for whom this is the only statutory right to be heard, can and ought to be expected to appreciate this is open to question.[11]

The Aims of Planning—Planners and the Courts

The purposes for which planning powers may be exercised are not specified by the Act which merely enjoins authorities to have regard to "the provisions of the development plan . . . and to any other material considerations" (*e.g.* section 29 (2)). It is for the courts to decide what considerations are "material." A Government decision is *ultra vires* and void if it is influenced by an improper purpose, or if irrelevant considerations are taken into account or relevant considerations not taken into account. The question of relevance is one of law (*Padfield* v. *Minister of Agriculture* [1968] A.C. 997).

Planning theorists have been much exercised by the search

for an ideology or a set of goals for planning. Unfortunately they do not seem to recognise that this is a legal question for the courts and assume that professional planners can determine their own goals. There has thus developed what has been described as "a messianic almost a megalomaniacal vision" by planners of their role in society (McAuslan (1974) 37 M.L.R. 134, 139). There can be few social and economic problems which cannot be related in some way to the use of land and thus the scope for discussing goals is virtually unlimited. Planners regard their function not merely as that of an umpire to resolve disputes over conflicting claims in respect of land use but as directors of the resources of their area. It has been maintained that planning powers can be used not merely for the negative purpose of preventing harmful activities, but the positive one of guiding social change. The planner has been described as "a helmsman steering the city" (see McLoughlin, *Urban and Regional Planning—A Systems Approach* (1969), pp. 83–87) and the position has been adopted that planning powers can be used to achieve any social or economic aim fettered only by the practical limitations of the development control machinery. Planning has also been called "a long step for balls which cannot be fielded by other public authorities" (Lichfield, *The Economics of Planned Development* (1956), p. 31).

The ambitious role in which planners have cast themselves is abhorrent to some lawyers who are concerned with the difficulty of exercising control over ill-defined powers. Lawyers have also pointed to practical difficulties inherent in a wide conception of planning. Thus where a large number of factors are taken into account in making a decision, the possibility of delay is greatly increased. Moreover generalised social and economic problems depend upon future events such as climate or birth rate which are either unforeseeable or in a liberal democracy outside the control of governments. Professional planners have developed elaborate techniques based upon presumed analogies between the social and the physical sciences for analysing facts and making predictions. These have produced their own technical terminology, *e.g.* "systems theory," "cybernetics," "feedback loops," "requisite variety," which isolate professional planners from both elected councillors and the general public thus increasing the difficulties of political as well as legal control.

Although in law the elected council is the decision maker, it is the officials appointed by the council to advise it who have the greater influence. There is general power to delegate decision-making to committees, sub-committees and officials (L.G.A. 1972, section 110 (2)). Moreover even without formal delegation the functions of collecting facts and making recommendations can always be performed by officials as long as the authority retains the power to overrule the recommendations (*R.* v. *Greater London Council*, *ex p. Blackburn* [1976] 1 W.L.R. 550).

Decision-making can be delegated in a variety of ways so as to preserve the overriding control of the council. Sometimes, for example, only decisions to *refuse* permission are delegated. Alternatively the council or the main committee may reserve the right to decide prescribed categories of case, for example those which are inconsistent with the development plan. Some councils have a procedure whereby any councillor can challenge a committee or sub-committee decision within a time limit (see Dobry, pp. 40–43). Decision-making is normally delegated to a committee but only exceptionally is there full delegation to officials.

A characteristic of local government committees is that officials and elected members participate on equal terms. However elected councillors are at a disadvantage *vis-à-vis* their professional advisers. Their part-time roles and relative lack of education coupled with the large number of applications make it difficult for them to assess the merits of the individual cases. In practice therefore the recommendations of officials are overruled only exceptionally.[12]

Where the committee does consider a particular case this is likely to be selected, not by virtue of its policy implications, but because it concerns the sort of detailed matter, often of a domestic or local kind, which lay councillors feel competent to discuss, or in respect of which individuals or local pressure groups have approached a council member (see Buxton, *Local Government* (2nd ed.), pp. 24–41).

Thus representative democracy is not an effective method of supervising development control decisions. It must also be remembered that there is no general requirement of public consultation in connection with development control (see p. 82, below) which comprises the largest area of governmental power where professional officials can in private and without statutory procedures for hearing persons affected, exercise wide discretions which directly affect individual freedom and property rights.

The claims of professional planners to play the part of social reformers have produced the doctrine known as *architectural determinism*. This presupposes that matters of physical layout and architectural design can in themselves produce changes in human behaviour. Adherents to this doctrine would use layout and design concepts for purposes of social engineering, and aspire to produce moral and social reforms, perhaps at the expense of more modest physical objectives such as comfort and convenience. Thus large shopping centres may be placed in new residential areas because of some *a priori* assumption by officials trained as social scientists, that a sense of community spirit is desirable, whereas on grounds of convenience and amenity smaller shops at dispersed locations might be preferred. Similarly bizarre forms of housing are sometimes provided to accommodate persons displaced from traditional communities by slum clearance schemes, upon the assumption that the former community ethos can thereby be preserved.[13]

Lawyers on the other hand have sometimes argued that the goals of planning should be narrowly conceived and confined to matters relating to "amenity" as defined by Scrutton L.J. in *Re Ellis* [1920] 1 K.B. 343, 370 to mean "pleasant circumstances or features, advantages" (see Heap, *The Land and The Development* (1975), pp. 41–48. On this view planning becomes a public law extension of the law of nuisance.[14]

An examination of the history of English planning law reveals that the purposes of the legislation have steadily widened. Planning legislation developed out of nineteenth-century Public Health Acts and thus its origins did indeed lie in the realm of the prevention of nuisance. The Housing, Town Planning, etc. Act of 1909 was wider in scope being concerned with amenity in the sense of pleasant as well as healthy surroundings and drawing its ideals from the residential estates owned and developed by benevolent industrialists for their workers, such as the Bournville estate in Birmingham and Port Sunlight on Merseyside.

After World War I it was more general social and economic problems such as the advent of the private motor car and the phenomen known as urban sprawl which led to further planning legislation. Unlike the 1909 Act this was not confined to building land but gave local authorities power to make planning schemes affecting their whole area (see Town and Country Planning Act 1932). At this stage of planning was still seen primarily as a local matter.

The stimulus for the general system of control introduced by the 1947 Act was a realisation of the interrelation between land use matters and general economic problems. There had been between the wars a drift of population towards the South East which resulted in congestion there and a decline in the economies of the older industrial areas of the north. There was in parts of Britain a serious erosion of agricultural land due to urban expansion and there was a need to modernise and to relocate industry and to deal with traffic congestion (see Barlow Report: Royal Commission on the Distribution of the Industrial Population, Cmnd. 6153 (1940) and Scott Report, Committee on Land Utilisation in Rural Areas, Cmnd. 6378 (1941)). It was thought essential that land use planning be treated as a national as well as a local matter. This was the decisive step from a narrow conception of planning. If amenity were to be the only concern of planning the most suitable decision-making organ would not be a political body but an independent and expert tribunal (see also Report of the Schuster Committee on the Qualifications of Planners, Cmnd. 8059 (1950)).

The 1968 Act confirmed this trend. The concept of a structure plan is consistent only with the assumption that planning concerns social and economic matters. Thus section 7 (4) requires the local planning authority to have regard to current policies with respect to the economic planning and development of the region as a whole (see also section 6). Indeed it is unrealistic to confine planning objectives to matters of amenity, unless it is assumed that there should be no governmental intervention of any kind in the economy. A problem which frequently arises in connection with land use concerns not amenity as such, but the balance to be achieved between amenity considerations on the one hand and on the other social and economic objectives such as trade and employment. To confine planning decisions to amenity would merely leave the final decision to be made elsewhere. Thus in the case of the application for planning permission to extend the Windscale nuclear fuel re-processing plant, an important issue was the extent to which an environmental hazard could be tolerated in return for economic benefits (see [1978] P.L. 218 for a convenient summary). However the political issues involved there were so unusually wide, including defence and international problems, that the normal planning machinery was insufficient. This was not because planning objectives are limited—a wide range of issues was discussed at the public inquiry—but because the quasi-judicial character of the public inquiry would, it was believed, preclude discussion of the issues in Parliament. The final decision was' eventually made by a ministerial order approved by Parliament (see p. 76, below).

Moreover, even if the extravagances of architectural determinism are disregarded it is plausible to believe that decisions made upon the basis of amenity have wider social implications which should be taken into account. Thus planning permission might be given for a low density, high amenity housing development which will attract only wealthy residents. This will have ramifications in the fields of transport, employment, education and leisure facilities as well as raising questions of distributive justice. In the United States, land use decisions taken for the lawful purpose of protecting local amenities have led to social problems where environmentally undesirable but socially necessary uses are restricted. Because of the narrow nuisance-orientated conception of the purposes of planning which has dominated United States law, the state courts have found it difficult to interefere with practises such as "snob," or "exclusionary" zoning (see Hagman, *Urban and Land Development* (1973), Chap. XVIII. Compare *R.* v. *Hillingdon Borough Council, ex p. Royce Homes Ltd*. [1974] Q.B. 720).

The English courts have not attempted to provide a general formula capable of indicating the purposes of planning legislation. This is hardly surprising in view of the casuistic approach taken by the judges to questions of statutory interpretation (*cf. Coleshill & District Investment Co.* v. *Minister of Housing* [1969] 1 W.L.R. 746). The court limits itself to deciding whether a particular consideration is relevant to the facts of the case before it.

Indeed the citizen who wishes to challenge a planning decision on the grounds of irrelevancy faces several problems arising out of the general law of judicial review.

First, he must establish *locus standi*. This is less difficult than is often assumed. It is true that a member of the public has insufficient standing to obtain a declaration that a planning decision is *ultra vires* (*Gregory* v. *Camden B.C.* [1966] 1 W.L.R. 899; *Simpson* v. *Edinburgh Corp.*, 1960 S.C. 313). A declaration will be only in favour of someone who can show that his legal position is altered because of the decision in question. The courts have sometimes allowed ratepayers to obtain declarations in respect of local authority decisions but the basis for this is an illegal expenditure out of the rates which effects the ratepayer because of the dubious proposition that the authority stands in a position analogous to that of a trustee in respect of the ratefund (*Prescott* v. *Birmingham Corporation* [1955] 1 Chap. 210). Unless compensation is payable for refusal of permission, this argument has no relevance in a planning context where expenditure of rates is not affected.

The same narrow concept of standing applied to mandamus (*R.* v. *Hereford Corp., ex p. Harrower* [1970] 1 W.L.R. 1424 although the position here is not free from doubt) and to the statutory procedure for challenging the appeal decision of the Secretary of State (see pp. 180–181, below).

However the order of certiorari has been held available to quash a planning decision (*R.* V. *Hillingdon B.C.*, above). The standing requirement for this remedy is generous. It is available in the court's discretion to any member of the public (*R.* v. *Thames Magistrates' Court, ex p. Greenbaum* (1957) 55 L.G.R. 129). The court will however refuse the remedy to a person who has no specific grievance or connection with the decision and intervenes only on behalf of the public interest[15] (compare *R.* v. *Bradford-on-Avon U.D.C.* [1964] 1 W.L.R. 1136 with *R.* v. *Hendon U.D.C., ex. p. Chorley* [1933] 2 K.B. 696 and see

Wade, p. 544). In *R.* v. *Sheffield City Council, ex. p. Mansfield,* (1979) 37 P. & C.R. 1, a ratepayer was permitted to apply for certiorari to quash a grant of planning permission for the use of a caravan site by gypsies. His application however failed on the merits (see further p. 85, below).)

The possibility of using certiorari applies only where a local authority decision is challenged. Judicial review of the Secretary of State's decision is governed by a statutory procedure where stricter principles apply (pp. 179–183, below).

Secondly there is a heavy burden of proof upon the applicant who must specifically allege the irrelevant factor which he claims to have been taken into account (*Cannock Chase D.C.* v. *Kelly* [1978] 1 W.L.R. 1). There is no general public access to government documents nor is there a general obligation to give reason for a decision. However under the General Development Order 1977, art. 7, an authority must give reasons for a refusal or a conditional grant of permission. A failure to do so does not however invalidate the permission (*Brayhead (Ascot) Ltd.* v. *Berkshire C.C.* [1964] 2 Q.B. 303; *cf. R.K.T. Investments Ltd.* v. *Hackney B.C.* [1978] E.C. 1915). Moreover the Secretary of State must give reasons for his appeal decision (Tribunals and Inquiries Act 1971, s. 12). Here a failure to give adequate reasons will entitle the court to quash the decision (see pp. 174–176, below).

No reasons need be given by a local authority for an unconditional grant of planning permission. Thus a person such as a local resident who wishes to contest it is at a disadvantage. The decision of the House of Lords in *Padfield* v. *Minister of Agriculture* [1968] A.C. 997 is sometimes cited as authority that where no reasons are given the court can infer that no proper reasons exist. This is an optimistic view of the case. The Minister there expressly gave an irrelevant reason for his decision and none of their Lordships would have been prepared to draw adverse inferences merely from a failure to give

reasons. Lord Morris dissented, the others limited themselves
to the proposition that a failure to give reasons does not in itself
exclude the power of the court, which can look at the effect of
the decision in the light of the circumstances measured against
the court's views of the scope of the governing legislation. "If all
the prima facie reasons seem to point in favour of . . . [the
Minister] taking a certain course . . . and he gives no reason
whatever for taking a contrary course the court may infer that
he has no good reason" (*per* Lord Pearce at p. 1053).

  In deciding what are the scope and purposes of a statutory
power the courts traditionally look at the statutory provisions
without recourse to statements of policy from other sources
such as the multitude of circulars issued by the Department of
the Environment (see *British Oxygen Co.* v. *Minister of
Technology* [1969] 2 Ch. 174. However there are signs that this
practice is becoming less strictly observed. *Coleshill & District
Investment Co.* v. *Minister of Housing* [1969] 1 W.L.R. 746
concerns the question whether demolition of a building
required planning permission. Lord Wilberforce relied *inter
alia* upon a long-standing practice endorsed by ministerial
circulars that planning permission was not required, and
suggested that this might rise to a form of customary law. It is
worth noting however that the ministerial view coincided with
the common law principle against interference with property
rights. And in *Bristol D.C.* v. *Clark* [1975] 1 W.L.R. 1443.
Scarman L.J. was prepared in a housing case to take account of
ministerial circulars as evidence of the policy of the legislation
(at p. 982). Again the circular supported the interests of the
individual. The courts have often been criticised on the grounds
that a judge is not qualified to define the aims of social
legislation and that they approach such questions with a bias in
favour of private property rights and against state intervention
(see Griffiths, *The Politics of the Judiciary* (1977)).

  Whether or not these criticisms are justified (see below,

p. 110) it is desirable that a judge should be required to consider the views of Ministers as to the aims of legislation. There need be no constitutional objection to this as long as the court is not bound by such views and can use them along with other techniques of statutory interpretation including the presumption against the deprivation of property right.[16]

The courts, perhaps influenced by the practice of planners, take a broad view of the purposes of planning and there are few cases where it has been held that irrelevant factors have actually been taken into account. Indeed in *Stringer* v. *Minister of Housing* [1970] 1 W.L.R. 1281) Cook J. thought that in principle any consideration relating to the use and development of land is capable to being a planning consideration. This topic will be discussed in Chapter 4.

Official Advice

We have already seen that officials exercise considerable influence upon decision-making. Problems arise when a statement made by an official conflicts with the decision ultimately taken by the authority. For example, a citizen may be informally told that he does not need planning permission only to find that the council subsequently takes enforcement proceedings. Assuming that the official has not warned him of this possibility, and that it is reasonable for him to rely upon the official's assurance there are two possible legal remedies open to him.

First, he may sue in tort upon the basis of a negligent misrepresentation by the official. It has been held that a duty of care can exist in respect of statements made by local authority employees exercising statutory functions (*Minister of Housing* v. *Sharp* [1970] 2 Q.B. 223). There is thus no need to establish that the official voluntarily assumed responsibility for his statement as would be the case in a private law context (see

Hedley Byrne & Co. Ltd. v. *Heller & Partners* [1964] A.C. 465; *Esso Petroleum* v. *Mardon* [1975] Q.B. 819). All loss which is reasonably foreseeable as a result of the official's assurance is recoverable in damages. This will normally be economic loss, caused for example by the purchase of equipment in connection with the development.

Secondly, he may argue that the official's representation binds the authority, so that they may not take enforcement action against him. This is more difficult and the cases conflict. However it is suggested that the problems have been caused by a failure to separate two distinct but related arguments, one based upon estoppel, the other upon delegation.

The most natural way of contending that an official assurance binds the authority is through the doctrine of estoppel. The citizen must show first that a statement of fact, or, in equity, a promise, was made by the official; secondly that it was reasonable for him to rely upon and that he did rely upon the statement; and thirdly that he incurred loss or detriment in acting upon the statement. Arguably this third requirement does not apply in case of equitable estoppel where the official makes a promise as opposed to a statement of fact (see *Alan* v. *El Nasr* [1972] 2 Q.B. 189. It may be necessary to show only that the promise was acted upon. This distinction may have merit in the private law context where it originated but in public law it serves no useful purpose. A public authority should not be bound by statements which cause no actual harm to the citizen. To distinguish for example between a statement that planning permission will be granted (promise) and one that planning permission is not required (fact) is to carry conceptualism to unacceptable lengths.

There is a fundamental objection to the estoppel argument. This is based upon the principle that a public authority cannot disable itself from exercising its statutory functions, nor can it increase its statutory powers by its own acts (see *Maritime*

Electric Co. v. *General Dairies* [1937] A.C. 610; *Rhyl U.D.C.* v. *Rhyl Amusements Ltd.* [1959] 1 W.L.R. 465). The responsibility for planning functions is vested in the council. Thus if the council is bound by statements of its officials the intention of Parliament is frustrated. This principle is often stated as the proposition that estoppel, consent or waiver cannot validate an *ultra vires* act, and was applied in *Southend Corporation* v. *Hodgson (Wickford) Ltd.* [1962] 1 Q.B. 416. There the Divisional Court held that the council was not bound by its engineer's erroneous assurance the respondents' proposed use as a builders yard did not need planning permission. The council's statutory discretion whether to take enforcement action was not to be hindered.

However there has been a judicial assault on this principle. In several cases, albeit in none was the point essential to the decision, it was held that estoppel can make an unauthorised decision binding upon an authority (*Robertson* v. *Minister of Pensions* [1949] 1 K.B. 227; *Lever Finance Ltd.* v. *Westminster Corp.* [1971] 1 Q.B. 222; *Norfolk County Council* v. *Secretary of State* [1973] 1 W.L.R. 1400) but *cf. Howell* v. *Falmouth Boat Construction Co.* [1951] A.C. 837). This line of cases provides an excellent illustration of the English courts' willingness to apply a private law concept, that of ostensible authority which derives from agency) to public law problems without discussion of the policy and conceptual problems thereby involved. Thus the public interest that planning decisions be made upon the basis of all relevant factors gives way to the interest of a private individual, an interest which in any event could inadequately be compensated by an action for damages. To allow estoppel a wide scope has two further undesirable consequences. It might prejudice the position of third parties such as neighbours in that a decision may become binding without compliance with statutory procedures designed to protect them. Secondly officials may be inhibited from giving informal advice by the

fear of binding their authority (see *Brooks & Burton* v.
Secretary of State (1976) 75 L.G.R. 285, 296).

The other line of argument based upon delegation is more
satisfactory. There is power to delegate planning to individual
officials. If there has been an express delegation the authority is
of course bound. It can be argued that even without an express
delegation, the authority may be bound if the citizen has
reasonably relied upon the ostensible authority of the official.
Evidence of the actual practice of the authority will establish
this. The absence of procedural formalities such as writing will
not invalidate the delegation because not all statutory
procedural requirements are regarded by the courts as essential
to validity. The courts distinguish between essential (mandatory) and non-essential (directory) requirements upon the
admittedly vague criterion of the importance of the provision in
question and in particular the consequences of disregarding it
(see below, p. 113 n.). Thus in *Wells* v. *Minister of Housing*
[1967] 1 W.L.R. 1000 a planning application was determined
by the authority without complying with non-essential formal
requirements. The decision was nevertheless held to bind the
authority. There is no reason why the doctrine of estoppel
should not apply in this limited context since there is no element
of *ultra vires* involved and thus no conflict of principle. Lord
Denning M.R. said in *Wells* at p. 1007, that "a public authority
cannot be estopped from doing its public duty, but I do think it
can be estopped from relying on technicalities." The requirements of the estoppel doctrine and in particular that of
reasonable reliance militate against any tendency to take this
too far. Strict adherence to formalities would produce "an
architect's nightmare and a bureaucrat's morass to the
advantage of nobody" (*per* Sachs L.J. in *Lever Finance* (above)
at p. 232) but on the other hand "the local planning authority is
not a free agent to waive statutory requirements in favour of (so
to speak) an adversary: it is the guardian of the planning

system" (*per* Russell L.J. (dissenting) in *Wells* at p. 1015).

This compromise approach was applied by Sachs L.J. in the *Lever* case although Lord Denning M.R. with whom Megaw L.J. agreed relied upon estoppel alone. An official informed the developer that certain variations in its plans would not require planning permission. There had been a long-standing practice to allow such decisions to be made by officials but on this occasion the council purported to overrule the official. It was held that the council was bound by the official's decision. However there was statutory power (Town and Country Planning Act 1968, s. 68) to delegate such matters to officers. No such power existed in 1962 when the *Southend* case was decided. The council had not delegated in writing as the Act required, but, on the basis of the *Wells* case, this could be treated as an inessential procedural requirement, the defect being cured by application of estoppel principles. No question of *vires* was therefore in issue.

Finally in *Western Fish Products Ltd. v. Penwith D.C.* (*The Times*, May 31, 1978) the Court of Appeal confined the operation of estoppel to situations first where there was power to delegate and where there had been delegation, and secondly to cases like *Wells* where minor procedural requirements were ignored. The doctrine that estoppel cannot fetter the exercise of a statutory discretion was reaffirmed. The case concerned a claim that the plaintiff was led to believe (during conversations) that it had existing use rights in respect of a proposed development. It was held on the facts that there had been neither a representation nor detrimental reliance. Moreover, the court doubted whether estoppel could be extended beyond situations involving the creation of proprietary interests over land (*sed quaere?*).

The views expressed about the general scope of estoppel were therefore *obiter*, and the conflict with *Lever Finance* remains (see also Ward [1978] J.P.L. 594).

The approach taken in *Western Fish* is to be preferred. It not only reconciles all the actual decisions if not the dicta, but is unobjectionable on policy grounds. A similar principle applies in company law (see *Royal British Bank* v. *Turquand* (1856) 6 E. & B. 327) and means that persons dealing with the authority need not concern themselves with whether internal procedures have been followed but only with the broad question of *vires*.

Notes

1 Previous Acts are the Town and Country Planning Act 1962; the Caravan Sites and Control of Development Act 1960, and the Town and Country Planning Act 1968. The relevant parts of these are consolidated in the 1971 Act.

2 See Barker, *The Civic Trust, The Local Amenity Movement* (Civic Trust 1976); also references to research in (1976) E.G. 345.

3 Compensation is payable in special cases regarded as involving exceptional hardship but which are of limited economic importance (see Heap, pp. 249–263). Moreover, if a landowner can show that the refusal of planning permission leaves his land incapable of "reasonably beneficial use in its existing state" he may compel the authority to buy his land from him. See generally Pts. VIII and IX of the 1971 Act; and McAuslan, Chap. 7, particularly pp. 602–636. Compensation is payable also in cases where an authority revokes a planning permission or prohibits the exercise of existing rights (section 45 and 51).

4 A study of the fortunes of the Land Commission Act 1967 is instructive in this connection.

5 The difference between this and the powers contained in the Community Land Act 1975 is that in the latter case acquisition need only be desirable as opposed to immediately necessary. The principle of a "land bank" is inherent in the community land scheme. It would be difficult in practice to justify the use of section 112 (1) (*d*) except as a supplementary power to section 123, which is much more restricted than the 1975 Act.

6 Until 1968 designation as a CDA was a condition precedent to the exercise of compulsory purchase powers under what is now section 112. However little use was made of the power to designate CDAs, because the Minister could not approve a CDA plan if he thought that compulsory requisition was unlikely to occur within 10 years.

7 There is also the opposite pitfall to be avoided of excessively detailed structure plans.

8 See Eddison and Earwicker, *Manpower for physical planning* (S.S.R.C., 1974).

9 Different arrangements apply in London. See Hamilton, pp. 23–26. There are also special provisions relating to National Parks, L.G.A. 1972, Sched. 17.

10 See *Code of Practice for Examinations in Public* (HMSO); also Bridges and Vielba: *Structure Plan Examination in Public; A Descriptive Analysis* (University of Birmingham). On structure plan consultation generally see McAuslan, pp. 97–113, 216–244; [1975] J.P.L. 516–627; [1973] J.P.L. 159; Cullingworth, pp. 259–263; Bridges [1978] J.P.L. 599.

11 See Local Plans: Public Local Inquiries—A guide to procedure, D.O.E. *cf.* Circular 55/77.

12 But *cf. Jeffs* v. *New Zealand Dairy Board* [1967] 1 A.C. 551, on the practice of rubber stamping recommendations. At present there are about 440,000 applications for planning permission per year. See *Development Control Statistics, 1975–76* (HMSO).

13 See Broady, *Planning For People*, pp. 74–177; also *New Society*, February 16, 1967.

14 It may be that the common law can do the job better. See *Miller* v. *Jackson* [1977] Q.B. 966.

15 Lack of individual standing can be cured by seeking the aid of the Attorney-General (see p. 4 above).

16 One objection to treating circulars as binding lies in the lack of publicity given to them. Some documents which are nominally circulars do however have legal effect as statutory "directions." See for example Town and Country Planning (Development Plans) Directions 1975; (*cf.* s. 31 (1)) of the 1971 Act. *Quaere* whether these should as sub-delegated legislation be treated as statutory instruments and thus published under the Statutory Instruments Act 1946. See Griffith and Street, *Principles of Administrative Law* (5th. ed.), pp. 52–63.

Chapter 2

DEVELOPMENT

"Development" has been described as a key word in the planners' vocabulary. This is because with some exceptions (see *e.g.* sections 51, 54–60, 63–65) planning controls can be exercised only in respect of activities which fall within the definition of development contained in section 22 of the Act.

The definition of development is of interest both for its practical importance and as an example of judicial creativity within a statutory régime. The statute itself provides little by way of definition and the judges have been required not only to explain what development means but also to produce supplementary concepts of their own in order to enable the concept of development to be used effectively. A clutch of novel jurisprudential entities has been introduced into our land law which may partly compensate those who regret the demise of such playthings as the legal contingent remainder, or the use upon a use.

Development is defined in section 22 (1) as "the carrying out of building, engineering, mining, or other operations in, on, over or under land" and "the making of any material change in the use of any buildings or other land." The two parts of this formula must be kept separate because "operational," as we will henceforward call it, and "change of use" development sometimes have different legal consequences (see *e.g.* below pp. 141–143). Section 22 goes on in subsections (2), (3) and (4) to give some specific cases. Those in subsection (2) "shall not be taken … to involve development." Those in subsections (3) and (4) are declared to constitute development.

It is important to mention the machinery for deciding whether development has taken place. The local planning authority may be called upon to decide whether development is proposed, either upon an application for planning permission under section 23 (1) or upon an application for a determination whether planning permission is required under section 53.[1] It may have to decide whether development has already taken place without permission in order to serve an enforcement notice under section 87 (1). In all three cases there is a right of appeal first to the Secretary of State and then to the High Court on a point of law. Alternatively, instead of appealing to the Secretary of State, the landowner can apply to the court for review of the local planning authority's decision (see below, pp. 107–111). There is thus an *embarras de richesse*. It has consistently been held, however, that the definition of development is basically a question of fact. Therefore the court is limited to deciding whether the local planning authority has applied the right criteria to the facts and it cannot interfere merely because in its opinion the right criteria have been wrongly applied, unless the decision is grossly unreasonable (see *Gray* v. *Oxfordshire C.C.* (1963) 15 P. & C.R. 1; *Howell* v. *Sunbury-on-Thames U.D.C.* (1963) 15 P. & C.R. 26; *Bendles Motors* v. *Bristol Corporation* [1963] 1 W.L.R. 247; *Braddon* v. *Secretary of State* [1977] J.P.L. 450). The need to allow the planning authority to decide in the first instance whether development has taken place has been emphasised both by the Court of Appeal (*Square Meals Frozen Foods Ltd.* v. *Dunstable Corporation* [1974] 1 W.L.R. 59, 65) and the House of Lords (*Pyx Granite Co.* v. *Ministry of Housing* [1960] A.C. 260.[2] Thus a landowner cannot apply to the court for a declaration as

c

to whether development is involved without first obtaining a ruling from the local planning authority.[3]

The meaning of "operational" and "change of use" development will be considered in turn, bearing in mind that the same activity, for example the conversion of a house into an office, may well constitute both. Nevertheless each must be treated separately. The two parts of the definition are conceptually distinct. Operational development implies some physical alteration to the land carried out by human beings. A material change of use can occur without any physical alteration to the land itself.[3]

"Building, Engineering, Mining or Other Operations"

This formula suffers, it has been said, from the lack of any common genus linking the three specified kinds of operation. Thus it was held in *Coleshill & Distrct Investment Co.* v. *Minister of Housing* [1969] 1 W.L.R. 746 that the *ejusdem generis* principle cannot be used to identify "other operations" although the looser *noscitur a sociis* principle could be invoked. Thus "other operations" are activities similar to any of the specified three where the ingenuity of the local planning authority cannot quite stretch the terms to meet the facts.

"Operation" refers to a human activity which physically "changes the character of the land" (*Cheshire C.C.* v. *Woodward* [1962] 2 Q.B. 126, *Parkes* v. *Secretary of State for the Environment and the Peak Park Planning Board*). Thus the "mischief" to which the provision is directed is the creation of environmental blemishes.

Coleshill & Distrct Investment Co. v. *Minister of Housing* is the leading decision on operational development, but unfortunately the House of Lords refused to lay down precise guidelines. Three notions were canvassed; first "change," which was regarded as too weak to be helpful; and secondly "positive construction," which elicited the most favourable response. This supports the governmental opinion that demolition of a building is not development (Circular 49/67). The third notion—that development is "what a developer does"—was rejected for obvious reasons. Such a formula would however have the advantage of excluding from the ambit of planning control many small activities carried on by a private householder, interference with which lays a planning authority open to accusations on the theme of petty bureaucracy.

The interpretation (section 290 (1)) provides that "building" includes "any structure or erection and any part of a building as so defined, but does not include plant or machinery comprised in a building." This is very wide. Any artificial object is a building as long as it is a "structure or erection." Size is immaterial (*Buckingham C.C.* v. *Callingham* [1952] 2 Q.B. 515). It is tempting to apply in this connection the common law rules relating to fixtures and there is authority supporting this approach (*Cheshire C.C.* v. *Woodward* (above)). It is difficult however to relate such an approach to the policy of planning legislation. Thus if a class of art students place a large, garishly-painted statue in front of their college premises this would not be a fixture (*Leigh* v. *Taylor* [1902] A.C. 157), but it is certainly something that a planning authority ought to control.

Anything which is a fixture for the purposes of the law of real property as being physically attached to the land and intended to be enjoyed as a permanent feature of that land would also be a "building" for planning purposes. Thus hoardings, radio masts and flagpoles have all been treated as buildings (see *Encyclopedia of Planning Law & Practice*, Vol. 4, pp. 6052–6053).

Where the object is not a fixture, as for example in the case of a mobile crane or a caravan, the correct approach is to determine the function fulfilled by the object and the extent to which it impinges on its surroundings (*Barvis* v. *Secretary of State* (1971) 22 P. & C.R. 710; see also *Cardiff Rating Authority* v. *Guest Keen Baldwin's Iron & Steel Co. Ltd.* [1949] 1 K.B. 385. Thus size, mobility and degree of permanence are relevant factors and it can be noticed that "environmental impact," as it is fashionable to call it, is the basis of this approach. Whether the particular operation is in fact undesirable on environmental grounds is not of course relevant until the stage of deciding whether to grant planning permission.

This test can be applied to the question whether parking a caravan constitutes development. This is usually treated, wrongly in the author's view, only as a material change of use (see *Guildford R.D.C.* v. *Penny* [1959] 2 Q.B. 112; *Hartnell* v. *Minister of Housing* [1965] A.C. 1134). It is thus commonly believed that it is not development for the owner of a dwelling-house to park his holiday caravan in his garden. The parking of a caravan within the curtilage of a dwelling-house will, as a material change of use, only be development if it is occupied as a living unit entirely independent of the house itself. Thus it will be immune from control if used to provide extra accommodation in connection with the house. This is somewhat unreal, since the effect on the neighbourhood is the same in both cases and it is difficult in these days of what are coyly referred to as mobile homes to make a significant planning distinction between constructing a wooden extension to a house and placing a caravan in the garden. Difficulties also arise under a change of use analysis where additional caravans are brought on to an existing caravan site. It is only exceptionally that an increase in the same activity will constitute development (see below, p. 56). These problems can be avoided by treating the parking of a caravan except on a purely temporary basis as a building operation. Indeed for rating purposes a caravan is sometimes treated together with the land itself as one unit of occupation, the degree of permanence being the test (see *Field Place Caravan Park Ltd.* v. *Harding* [1966] 2 Q.B. 484).

Returning to the meaning of "operation," it is clear that placing a building on land constitutes development and it is provided that "building operation" includes alterations to and renovation of a building as well as "other operations normally undertaken by a person carrying on business as a builder" (section 290 (1)). It is difficult to envisage anything done to a building that could not be described as putting it up, altering it or taking it down. It may be that the phrase is intended to catch preparatory activities such as levelling a site, but these can anyway be regarded as engineering operations.

One important exception should be noticed here. Under section 22 (2) "works for the maintenance improvement or other alteration of any building" are not development providing that they affect only the interior of the building or do not affect its external appearance. If we follow literally the interpretation section's instruction that "building" includes part of a building (section 290 (1)), then nothing can fall within this provision. We must therefore fall back, as the context obviously demands, on a more restricted definition of building which it can be suggested means a structure providing accommodation whether for humans, animals or chattels. It is a question of degree for the planning authority whether a particular activity is merely an alteration, as opposed to a rebuilding, which requires permission, even where the replacement is to the same specifications as the original (*Street* v. *Essex C.C.* (1965) 193 E.G. 537).[4] Thus where a house is burned down any subsequent rebuilding will require planning permission. Moreover to see whether there has been any change in external appearance the end product must be compared with the appearance of the building immediately before the relevant operations began. Thus the restorer of a derelict country cottage cannot claim the benefit of the

exception. Indeed even the residential use right in such a
cottage is likely to have been lost by abandonment (see below,
pp. 58–60).

The most notorious query in the definition of development
and an examination question chestnut, is whether demolition
constitutes development.

In *Coleshill & District Investment Co.* v. *Minister of Housing*
[1969] 1 W.L.R. 746 the House of Lords held that the
demolition of earthworks surrounding a disused dump was
development. This was on the basis alternatively that the
large-scale shifting of materials constituted an engineering
operation, or that, treating the whole complex as a single entity,
this was an external alteration to a building.

Their Lordships were not prepared to say whether
demolition *per se* could be development. They took the view
that the issue thus formulated was too wide. "Demolition," like
"modernisation," can cover a wide variety of fact situations.
The correct approach was to examine the facts of each case to
see whether they fitted the language of section 22. Their
Lordships did however incline towards the view that development implies a positive act, not something destructive. Given
that one function of the highest appellate tribunal is to clarify
points of principle, was not this approach excessively cautious?
It is difficult to see how demolition can be thought of as
equivalent in vagueness to terms like modernisation.

However, apart from *Coleshill* there are dicta from the Court
of Appeal in favour of the view that demolition is not
development (*Iddenden* v. *Secretary of State* [1972] 1 W.L.R.
1433; *Howell* v. *Sunbury-on-Thames U.D.C.* (1963) 15 P. &
C.R. 26; see also *L.C.C.* v. *Marks & Spencer Ltd.* [1953] A.C.
535).

The arguments in support of this are unconvincing. There is
nothing in the notion of a building operation to restrict its
natural meaning to positive acts. If partial demolition is

development is there any reason to treat total demolition differently? It is true that in material change of use cases the cessation of a use is not development unless replaced by another use (see below, pp. 58–60). To hold otherwise would raise enforcement problems, since a person cannot be forced to be active. This does not apply to demolition cases. Restoration of a building can reasonably be required by an enforcement notice, bearing in mind that a planning authority can "under enforce" by requiring less than full restoration (see below, p. 147). It is sometimes suggested that the specific prohibitions in sections 54–58 against the demolition of buildings listed as of special historic or architectural interest show that demolition generally is not to be controlled. This is fallacious. The controls over listed buildings equally prohibit external alterations to them, which do constitute development. It is moreover a criminal offence *per se* to demolish a listed building (section 55). This is not the case with ordinary development. The listed building controls are thus more stringent supplements to the general law and have no necessary connection with the concept of development.

Finally as Dobry pointed out (*Control of Demolition* (1974), demolition raises significant environmental problems and thus in the absence of necessary statutory implication and binding authority it is suggested that it should always be regarded as development. Fears of undue infringement by the planners upon individual freedom can be allayed by granting permission under a general development order for harmless activities such as the demolition of domestic outbuildings.

It is relevant to note that for the purpose of the Factories Act 1961 "building operation" expressly includes the demolition of a building. The clear and comprehensive definition of building operation contained in section 76 (1) of that Act could with advantage be adopted by the draftsmen of the planning legislation.

Because of the wide meaning of "building," many activities normally regarded as engineering operations could equally be treated as building operations, for example the construction of bridges. Engineering is a heterogeneous term, but its meaning must be limited by the context ("in, on, over or under land"), to what is known as civil engineering—activities which involve physical alteration to the land itself. The context here displaces the interpretation section principle that "land" includes buildings. The removal of the earthworks in the *Coleshill* case was treated as an engineering operation, as could be the infilling of a pit, the making of a swimming pool, and the laying out of a golf course.

Mining operations are also undefined, but the interpretation section gives the word "mineral" a sufficiently wide meaning (". . . all substances . . . of a kind ordinarily worked for removal by underground or surface working, except peat cut for purposes other than sale") to permit the removal of any substance from the land to be treated as a mining operation with the probable limitation that "substance" excludes living things. Digging up a treee is not therefore a mining operation, and the Act provides special controls in respect of trees (sections 59–60). A problem analogous to that in the case of building operations arises in that the removal of substances from a spoil heap may not constitute mining if the heap is regarded as a chattel. Ministerial decisions have applied a functional test, so that the heap will cease to be a chattel if it has visually merged with the landscape by becoming, for example, overgrown (see [1950] J.P.L. 437; [1952] J.P.L. 58–165).

An operation is essentially a physical act. In the case of mining operations it has been held in *Thomas David (Porthcawl)* v. *Penybont R.D.C.* [1972] 1 W.L.R. 1526 that each "bite" of the shovel constitutes a separate operation for the purposes of the "four-year rule" under which an enforcement notice must be served within four years of the commencement of the operation in question. This analysis does not however apply to a building operation such as the construction of a house, where each individual act has meaning only as a contribution to a single end product. Thus in *Copeland B.C.* v. *Secretary of State for the Environment* (1976) 31 P. & C.R. 403 planning permission was granted for the building of a house. An enforcement notice subsequently treated the failure to construct the roof according to specifications as a separate act of development. It was held that this was a breach of planning control in respect of the whole house, which was a single operation and the notice was therefore invalid. Lord Widgery C.J. pointed out that to divide the various acts involved in house-building into separate operations would lay open the way to all manner of eccentric omissions by builders.

Material Change of Use

This aspect of development has given rise to much litigation. The central problem is to establish when a change becomes "material." Any variation in the activities carried out on land is a change in the use of that land. Not all such variations will be material and require planning permission. The word "material" has in the present context three separate meanings—first "physical," as opposed to mental. A subjective change in the purposes of an occupier will not in itself constitute development. Thus where car repairs previously carried out as a hobby were continued on a commercial basis, this was not development without a physical change, such as a marked increase in the level of activity (*Peake* v. *Secretary of State for Wales* (1971) 22 P. & C.R. 889; see also *Snook* v. *Secretary of State for the Environment* (1977) 33 P. & C.R. 1). The mental element is not however entirely irrelevant (see below, pp. 58–59).

Secondly "material" means substantial. Trivial changes of use will be ignored for planning purposes (see below, pp. 62–63).

Thirdly "material" means relevant. This is crucial. There is ample authority that a change of use is material only if it is the sort of change that raises considerations relevant to the purposes of planning legislation, for example whether it will affect the amenities of the neighbourhood or impose an additional burden upon public facilities (*East Barnet U.D.C.* v. *British Transport Commission* [1962] 2 Q.B. 484; *Marshall* v. *Nottingham Corporation* [1960] 1 W.L.R. 707; *Devon C.C.* v. *Horton* (1963) 81 L.G.R. 60, 63; *Devon C.C.* v. *Allen's Caravans (Estates) Ltd.* (1963) 61 L.G.R. 57, 58; *Guildford R.D.C.* v. *Penny* [1959] 2 Q.B. 112; *Miller* v. *Minister of Health* [1968] 1 W.L.R. 992).

Three general points can be made. First, if a change of use does not *in itself* raise planning considerations, it is not "material" merely because the new activity is carried on in such a way as to cause harm to the amenities of the area. Thus in *Marshall* v. *Nottingham Corporation* (above) land previously used for the manufacture and sale of garden huts became used for the sale of garden equipment not manufactured on the premises. Part of the land was flattened and cleared of trees so that the site was no longer screened from the public view. It was held that there was no material change in the use of the land. The change in what was sold was not relevant from the planning point of view and the detriment to local amenity was caused by the felling of the trees and therefore unrelated to the change as such.

Secondly, as in the case of operational development, it is irrelevant whether the change is in fact undesirable. What matters is that the change is of a kind which in principle raises planning considerations.

Thirdly, the definition section draws a clear distinction between operational and change of use development. Section 290

(1) provides that, " 'use' in relation to land does not include the use of land for the carrying out of any building or other operations thereon."

It is curious that the section makes no reference to engineering or mining operations. In *Parkes* v. *Secretary of State* [1979] 1 All E.R. 211, the Court of Appeal left open the question whether these operations could in some circumstances also constitute a use. That case concerned the question whether the placing of scrap metal upon land constituted a use of that land so as to be capable of forming the subject of a discontinuance (see section 55 1 (1) (*a*)). Their Lordships held that the general scheme of the act was to distinguish between the two halves of the definition of development and that the activity in question constituted a use and not an operation.

Attempts have been made to formulate general concepts in order to explain what is a material change. The phrase "changing the character of the land" is often employed. This seems to mean no more than that the change must be substantial (but see below, p. 57).

Sometimes a distinction is made between a change in "kind" and a change in "degree," the former being said always to involve development (see Circular 67/49). The concept of a change in "kind" appears to mean only that a different label can be attached as a matter of language to the new activity. It is doubtful however whether the subtle nuances of the English tongue bear any necessary relationship to distinctions relevant to a planner. There is a world of social distinction between "Tea Room" and "Snack Bar," but it is unlikely that a change in nomenclature made in order to attract a classier clientèle would justify the intervention of a planning authority. Changes in "kind" are moreover relative, since the classification of "kinds" varies with the point of view of the classifier. Thus a newsagent and a pornographic bookshop are both shops of the same kind to the person searching for a chemist, whereas a policeman would classify the facts differently. The identification of a change in "kind" is therefore merely a way of stating a conclusion that a given change is relevant from the point of view of planning policy.

Perhaps the most common approach is through the classical *per genus et speciem* principle. Broad categories of use are identified—residential, commercial, industrial, recreational, etc. and these are subdivided into more detailed categories—shops, light industrial, office, cinema and so on. However the Act gives no evidence as to how far this process should be taken before a change becomes too slight to be "material." The fundamental problem in change of use cases is to establish the level of generality at which the facts should be analysed. The process of subdivision can be extended indefinitely.

Any human activity can in theory be called a "use" of land. For example it is likely that a hotel which introduces a public discothèque is involved in a material change of use, but if topless dancers are later introduced, can the planning authority by calling this a "use" of land, validly claim that planning permission is required? The distinction between "kind" and "degree" does not provide a reliable tool of analysis, but it may be relevant as a prima facie approach. Thus it has sometimes been held that a detailed change within a broad category is not development, as in *East Barnet U.D.C.* v. *British Transport Commission* [1962] 2 Q.B. 484, where a yard previously used for the storage of coal to be transported by rail was held not to undergo development when it became used for the storage of crated cars, also to be transported by rail.

Other cases show the danger of relying on this approach. In *Birmingham Corporation* v. *Habib Ullah* [1964] 1 Q.B. 178, the Minister, in dealing with a case involving an increase in the number of families occupying a dwelling-house, thought that because the premises remained "residential" there could be no material change of use. It was held that the facts could be examined in detail and that development may occur if for example a dwelling-house became a house "let in lodgings." Such a distinction may raise planning issues[5] and is therefore "material."

It is instructive to compare the facts of *Marshall* v. *Nottingham Corporation* (above, p. 52) with those of *Williams* v. *Minister of Housing* (1967) 18 P. & C.R. 514. In the former case land previously used both for the manufacture and sale of garden equipment became used for the sale of garden equipment not manufactured on the premises. This was held not to be a material change because the broad category of activity remained the same. In *Williams* the land was used as a market garden and a hut on the site was used for the retail sale of produce from the garden. It was held that where imported oranges were sold from the hut (amounting to about 10 per cent. of the business) a material change of use took place. *Williams* has been criticised (see Palk (1973) 37 Conv. (N.S.) at pp. 185–186), but it is consistent with *Marshall*. There is a difference from the point of view of planning policy between a landowner selling the produce of his own land and retail sales generally, because the encouragement of local horticulture is a legitimate concern of a planner. The introduction of sales from outside could be the thin end of an unwanted wedge. In the case of the sale of garden huts it was no concern to the planner that these were not manufactured on the site (see also *Bromley (London Borough of)* v. *Haeltschi* [1978] J.P.L. 45). Thus facts can be analysed in any degree of detail to discover considerations relevant to planning policy (*cf. Hussain* v. *Secretary of State* (1971) 23 P. & C.R. 330).

Other generalisations have also turned out to be unreliable.

In *Lewis* v. *Secretary of State* (1971) 23 P. & C.R. 125 it was said that a change in the identity of an occupier cannot in itself constitute a material change in the use of the land where the activities carried out remain the same. This proposition will normally hold good, but occasionally the identity of the occupier will be relevant to planning policy. Thus in *Wilson* v. *West Sussex C.C.* [1963] 2 Q.B. 764 the Court of Appeal held that the phrase "agricultural cottage" denoted a cottage intended to be inhabited by agricultural workers. Danckwerts and Diplock L.JJ. took the view that if the cottage became occupied by non-agricultural workers a material change in the use of the land would take place. The rationale of this is similar to that in *Williams*. The preservation of agricultural land unpolluted by urban influences is a legitimate aspect of planning policy as is the need for agricultural workers to live near their work (*cf. East Suffolk C.C.* v. *Secretary of State* (1972) 70 L.G.R. 595.)[6]

Once it is accepted that changes which raise questions of planning policy are "material" then cases concerning the doctrine of "intensification" raise no particular difficulty. There are numerous authorities, albeit mostly in the form of *obiter dicta* (see *e.g.* the *East Barnet*, *Marshall* and *Penny* cases cited above, and *Brookes* v. *Flintshire C.C.* (1956) 6 P. & C.R. 140) in favour of the proposition that a marked increase in the same activity can constitute development. In *de Mulder* v. *Secretary of State* [1974] Q.B. 792 the court took the view that whatever the objections to the principle the authorities are now too strong to be overcome. In the *Guildford* case (above, p. 52) it was held that an intensification could amount to development if it introduced new planning problems to the land. Thus safety, and the need for additional services, would be factors in deciding whether an increase in the number of caravans on a caravan site would constitute development. Indeed in the *Guildford* case Lord Evershed M.R. referred to an intensification resulting in a change in the "character" of the land, by which he apparently meant a lowering of social tone. This approach, apart from being over politically thin ice, raises difficult problems of enforcement if extended to changes in "tone" caused by factors less concrete than intensification. Does development take place for example when a district of mean terraced houses originally inhabited by poor families becomes fashionable and is "colonised" by affluent persons with genteel pretensions?

There are few cases, however, where intensification was held on the facts to constitute development (see *James* v. *Secretary of State for Wales* [1966] 1 W.L.R. 135; (see *Chrysanthou* v. *Secretary of State* for the Environment and London Borough of Haringey [1976] J.P.L. 371; *Brooks & Burton Ltd.* v. *Environment Secretary* [1978] 1 All. E.R. 733; *Hilliard* v. *Secretary of State* [1978] J.P.L. 41). In *Marshall* v. *Nottingham Corporation* (above) it was thought that something "over-whelming" would be required.

Commentators sometimes treat as examples of intensification cases which are analytically quite distinct. These concern an activity originally ancillary to another use, and therefore not in law a "use" at all, which increases to become independent of the parent use and is thereby converted into use in its own right (see below, p. 61). Thus in *Jones* v. *Secretary of State* (1974) 28 P. & C.R. 362 workshops had been used for the manufacture of tractors in connection with the appellant's road haulage business. On the termination of the haulage business the manufacturing use was increased and work was taken on from outside. It was held that a material change of use had occurred, not by way of intensification but because the manufacturing use had become independent of the main haulage use. This was thus a case of a change between the main haulage use and a legally new manufacturing use (compare *Snook* v. *Secretary of State* (1977) 33 P. & C.R. 1).

There is therefore considerable flexibility within the concept of material change of use. It is for example sometimes thought that the planning authority cannot intervene where there is a modification of an industrial process so that it becomes more hazardous unless "operations" are involved in the modification or a change in the end product. This is fallacious. Safety is certainly a legitimate planning consideration (*Hidderley* v. *Warwickshire C.C.* (1963) 61 L.G.R. 266; *Stringer* v. *Minister of Housing* [1970] 1 W.L.R. 1281). Thus a change which takes the form of burning a new fuel could be held to be material. Indeed in *Gray* v. *Oxfordshire County Council* (1963) 15 P. & C.R. 1 the Divisional Court thought that it was not possible to separate the notion of "kind" of activity from the methods by which that activity is carried out.

Development occurs when a change takes place. It is thus necessary to identify the time when this occurs. It is clear that "use" is in law a notional concept which does not necessarily correspond to the physical facts on the land. We have already met one example of this in the case of the ancillary use, under which for example a block of offices serving a factory will have an industrial rather than an office use. Moreover a use may still adhere in law to the land even if all activities on the land have ceased (see below, p. 59). What evidence will establish that the land has in law a particular use? A mental act alone is not sufficient. It is also clear that the use need not be fully implemented in the sense that activities associated with it are actually being pursued on the land. Thus in *Peake* v. *Secretary of State for Wales* (1971) 22 P. & C.R. 889 a building which was not yet in use was held to have a use as a garage by virtue only of its design. It is suggested therefore that it is sufficient to show first an intention and secondly the existence of facts consistent, but not necessarily exclusively so, with that intention.

The converse situation of the discontinuance of a use can now be examined. There are two situations. First a use can be abandoned. Thus in *Hartley* v. *Minister of Housing* [1970] 1 Q.B. 413 a site had a dual use as a petrol filling station and for car sales. Owing to ill health the occupier ceased the car sales side of the business. Five years later car sales were resumed by a subsequent occupier. It was held that this resumption was a material change in the use of the land. The Court of Appeal laid down some important propositions. First, cessation of a use is not in itself development. Secondly, if a use has been abandoned then it ceases to exist whether it is replaced by another or left unused. Thirdly, the resumption of an abandoned use constitutes a material change of use. Enforcement problems explain why the logically identical situation of a change from a positive to a nil use is not regarded as constituting development.

Where however land is disused but its previous use is not abandoned, then the previous use remains effective. The Court of Appeal held that abandonment is a question of fact and that evidence of intention is crucial. As formulated by Lord Denning M.R. the position seems to be analogous to the case of abandonment of domicile of choice in the conflict of laws (see *Re Flynn* [1969] 2 Ch. 403). Thus two elements are required, a factual cessation of activity and the absence of an intention to resume at any specific time. Thus if in *Hartley* the previous occupier had shown an intention to recommence the selling of cars when her husband's health improved the use might have been preserved.

The court saw the matter in terms of a presumption in favour of abandonment which grows in strength proportionately to the length of time the land is disused. A positive intention not to resume will however constitute abandonment but only if it is unequivocal. Thus receiving, but not implementing, a planning permission for another use, or offering the premises for sale, would not suffice.

Secondly a use can be terminated by operation of law. Here intention is normally irrelevant. There are two kinds of case. First, where one use is replaced by another inconsistent use the first use is brought to an end and cannot be kept notionally alive by showing an intention to resume (*Grillo* v. *Minister of Housing* (1968) 208 E.G. 1201; *Postill* v. *East Riding C.C.* [1956] 2 Q.B. 386). Even if the second use is only temporary, the resumption of the previous use will be development.

There is one special case. It was held by the Court of Appeal in *Webber* v. *Minister of Housing* [1968] 1 W.L.R. 29 that where there is a regular cycle of activities on a site viewed over a substantial period of time, as in the case of a seasonal alteration between agricultural and camping uses, then each use can be regarded as an existing use of the land. Thus the cyclical altera-tion between them would not constitute development. It is as if they co-existed simultaneously. It is perhaps difficult to recon-cile this reasoning with the basic statutory premise that what is forbidden is a *change* in a use and not a use in itself but the practical advantage of the *Webber* principle is obvious.

A use is also lost where a building is erected on a site on which the use is carried out. In *Petticoat Lane Rentals Ltd.* v. *Secretary of State* [1971] 1 W.L.R. 1112 it was held that the erection of an office block on stilts over a site previously used by market traders extinguished the "market" use of the site, even though the market could still physically have been carried on beneath the building. The rationale is that the erection of the building creates an entirely new planning unit and wipes out entirely the previous history of the site, so that in planning terms there is a new piece of land with a nil use.[7] It seems however that the use is extinguished only in respect of the land actually covered by the new building. Thus in *Hilliard* v. *Secretary of State* (1977) 34 P. & C.R. 193 a site was used partly for agricultural purposes and partly for sale of produce from other sources. It was held that the use of a new building on the site could be limited without reference to any use rights existing on the surrounding land, thus presupposing that such rights still existed.[8]

Multiple Uses

We have discussed the general nature of a material change in the use of land. The courts have developed special principles to deal with the situation where more than one use exists on a site.

There are again two kinds of case. First, there may be one or more main uses together with other related uses which are subordinate and incidental to a main use. These uses are called "ancillary." They are not recognised as uses in their own right but will in law partake of whatever is their "parent" use. Thus in *Trentham* v. *Gloucestershire C.C.* [1966] 1 W.L.R. 506, where a building on a farm was used for the storage of agricultural equipment, the use of the whole site was held to be agricultural with no "storage" element. The Court of Appeal held that when the building became used for the storage of builders' materials a material change of use had taken place from "agricultural" to "storage." A feature of this kind of case is that the legal use of the ancillary activity may change without any physical change in the activity itself, for example if the part of the premises originally used for the major use is used for something else (see *Jones* v. *Secretary of State* (above); *Clarke* v. *Minister of Housing* (1967) 18 P. & C.R. 82). Conversely the physical activity may change quite drastically without there being a material change of use. If in the case above, the building used for storing farm equipment was turned over to growing mushrooms the use in law would remain agricultural (*cf. Brazil Concrete* v. *Amersham R.D.C.* (1967) 18 P. & C.R. 396; *Vickers Armstrong* v. *Central Land Board* (1957) 9 P. & C.R. 33).

An ancillary use proper may be compared with the case where a second use on a site is unrelated to the main use but is too small, sporadic or temporary to be regarded as "material" (see *Biss* v. *Smallburgh R.D.C.* [1965] Ch. 335). This situation differs from that of the ancillary use proper in one respect. If the parent use ceases, an ancillary use will become a use in its own right and development may occur. The cessation of the major use will not affect the status of the insubstantial use which can always be ignored.

One ministerial application of the ancillary use doctrine is dubious. In Circular 67/49 the Minister stated that he would not treat as a material change of use a situation where a "professional man—say a doctor or a dentist" uses rooms in a private dwelling for consultation purposes. Not only has this principle been applied arbitrarily, as where use of part of a dwelling-house for a tailoring business, and by an architect for professional purposes were both treated as development (see [1970] J.P.L. 674), but the Circular itself appears to be misconceived. Use as a doctor's surgery has no functional connection with use as a dwelling-house and is thus not ancillary. It makes nonsense of the doctrine to hold that merely because two uses are conveniently operated on the same site one is ancillary to the other. The use of part of a doctor's dwelling-house as a surgery is properly treated as the introduction of a separate independent use, and falls within the second category of case.

This is where a site has more than one independent use. Here both uses whether or not geographically separated are the normal uses of the site and each must be looked at separately to determine whether development has taken place. There is one special feature of this class of case. This is where one of two concurrent uses ceases thereby enabling the other one to expand and to absorb the whole of the land occupied by the defunct use. If this occurs a material change of use takes place (*Wipperman* v. *Barking Borough Council* (1965) 17 P. & C.R. 225), and it makes no difference whether the uses were physically intermingled or separate. This principle has been criticised (see Palk (1973) 33 Conv. 168), but it is suggested that it is merely an example of the operation of ordinary principles. In *Bromsgrove D.C.* v. *Secretary of State for the Environment* [1978] J.P.L. 747, Forbes J. regarded the *Wipperman* principle as an example of intensification and applicable only where the encroaching use absorbs the whole site. This is inconsistent with the earlier decision in *Brooks* v. *Gloucestershire C.C.* (1967) 66 L.G.R. 386, where part of a dwelling-house was used as a shop, the shop part later encroaching into the territory of the dwelling-house. It was emphasised that the principle is not based upon intensification but upon displacement. This analysis is desirable from a policy point of view, since the balance of uses on a site may raise planning issues. Thus if one half of a large field was used for grazing, the other as a sports field, and the uses were switched around so that sports now take place in what was hitherto the grazing area, then this should be regarded as development so that the switch can be prevented if, for example, an adjoining housing estate would be adversely affected. There is clearly no question of intensification in such a case.

The Unit of Development

Before deciding whether development has taken place the authority must identify the unit of land in relation to which the facts must be analysed. The most natural unit and the one applicable in the majority of cases is the area occupied by a single occupier or by joint occupiers in a common enterprise. If some other unit is chosen then this may produce a different result. Thus in *James* v. *Secretary of State for Wales* [1966] 1 W.L.R. 135 part of a site was occupied by caravans and planning permission was sought for an increase in the number of vehicles so as to encroach on to another part of the site. If the appropriate unit was the land actually covered by caravans, then encroachment on to neighbouring land would constitute a change in the use of that land. If however the whole site occupied by the developer could be considered the problem becomes one of intensification and it would be more difficult to establish development.

The unit problem also arises in connection with enforcement notices. Thus in *Thomas David (Porthcawl) Ltd.* v. *Penybont R.D.C.* [1972] 1 W.L.R. 1526 mining operations took place only on part of the unit occupied by the developer. Nevertheless it was held that an enforcement notice could validly prohibit the extension of operations over the rest of the unit.

The unit problem has been discussed most frequently in connection with cases involving multiple user. Thus in *Williams* v. *Minister of Housing* (above, p. 55) if the hut were to be regarded as a separate unit then development could not have taken place since at all relevant times retail sales would have been the use of that unit. A use cannot be "ancillary" to activities outside its own unit.

The law governing identification of the unit of development is now reasonably clear (see *Burdle* v. *Secretary of State for the Environment* [1972] 1 W.L.R. 1207; *Wood* v. *Secretary of State for the Environment* [1973] 1 W.L.R. 707; *Johnston* v. *Secretary of State for the Environment* (1974) 28 P. & C.R. 424; *Wakelin* v. *Secretary of State for the Environment* [1978] (*The Times*, June 11). As usual the question is primarily one of fact for the planning authority who must direct their attention to two possible units. The primary unit is the whole area occupied by the developer. The nature of his estate or interest in the land is not relevant.

In all cases there is a presumption, which is particularly strong in the case of a dwelling-house, that the unit of occupation is also the unit of development. This has been the unit chosen in the overwhelming majority of cases. The presumption can be rebutted if there are separate "units of activity" within the primary unit. Where it can be shown that there are areas, geographically distinct, in which activities unrelated to those on adjoining areas are carried out, then these areas can be treated as separate planning units. The most common example arises where part of an area of land is used as a caravan site and the rest for agricultural purposes (see *James* v. *Secretary of State for Wales*, [1968] A.C. 409; *R.* v. *Axbridge R.D.C.* [1964] 1 W.L.R. 442; *Williams-Denton* v. *Watford R.D.C.* (1963) 61 L.G.R. 423; *Hartnell* v. *Minister of Housing*, [1965] A.C. 1134). It will be a question of fact in each case whether the caravan site is sufficiently distinct geographically to be treated separately. Such matters as the existence of fences and similar boundaries are of evidential value. In "ancillary use" cases there is no separate "unit" problem since if a use is ancillary to another use within the same area of occupation the whole will, *ipso facto*, comprise a single unit of development. Unrelated uses however will not produce separate units without sufficient degree of geographical separation. Thus in *Brooks* v. *Gloucestershire C.C.* (1967) 66 L.G.R. 386) where part of a manor house was used as a shop and restaurant, the whole was treated as a single unit even though the commercial activities were confined to certain rooms. This can be explained on the basis of the strong presumption against subdividing a dwelling-house, in the light particularly of a small amount of intermingling of domestic use within the room used for the business. However *Brooks* does show the danger of over-emphasising the importance of the conceptual "unit" question. In *Brooks* it made no difference which of the two possible units was selected. This is because of the *Wipperman* principle that encroachment by one use on to the territory of another is, in itself, a material change of use (see above, p. 62). Thus even if the shop part of the house had been treated as a separate unit, development would still have taken place when this extended into the residential part.

Even in intensification and enforcement notice cases, it will be very rare that a unit other than that of occupation is selected and rarer still that it will be decisive. It is suggested that in order to avoid multiplying concepts it would be preferable in all cases to have regard only to the area of occupation. The contrary authorities consist mainly of *obiter dicta*. Indeed judicial statements can be found which seem to assume that the area of occupation is indeed the only appropriate unit (*Brazil Concrete Ltd.* v. *Amersham R.D.C.* (1967) 18 P. & C.R. 396, 399; *Vickers-Armstrong* v. *Central Land Board* (1957) 9 P. & C.R. 33, 37; but see Palk 37 Conv. (N.S.) at pp. 174–176 for criticisms of this approach).

However in *Kwick Save Ltd.* v. *Secretary of State* (1979) 37 P. & C.R. 170, a complex of buildings was originally used in connection with a garage business. One building was later occupied by a separate concern, planning permission having previously been granted for retail purposes but without specifying the type of goods to be sold. The issue was whether the planning permission authorised the use of the building as a supermarket. The unit of activity principle was applied and it was held that the complex remained a single planning unit. Thus the building could only be used for the sale of goods connected with the garage and not as a general supermarket.

This is a novel application of the unit doctrine. First, the notice of a unit of activity has hitherto been used only to subdivide land occupied by a single occupier. Here land controlled by separate occupiers is being welded into a single unit. The practical difficulties inherent in this principle are obvious. Secondly the reasoning appears to be circular, since the conclusion that there is a single unit of activity is feasible only upon the basis that the planning permission joined the use of the shop to that of the garage; indeed this case reveals the superfluity of the unit of activity principle since the same result could have been achieved by treating the shop as a separate unit and attaching a condition to the planning permission limiting its use to the sale of motoring accessories.

Special Cases

Acts which are not development

Section 22 (2) lists six acts which "shall not be taken to involve development of the land."

One of these we have already noticed. This is an alteration to a building which affects only its interior or which does not materially affect the external appearance (see above, p. 47). This concession has been slightly modified in that *underground* extensions to a building commenced after December 5, 1968 are excluded and thus being clearly an alteration to the land do constitute development.

Two more concern routine maintenance work of public authorities (see Appendix).

The fourth exception, "use within the curtilage of a dwelling-house for any purpose incidental to the enjoyment of the dwelling-house as such," is superfluous in the light of the development by the courts of the doctrine of the ancillary use (above, p. 61). However, its inclusion does cast doubt upon the validity of the courts' approach, since it indicates that the notion of ancillary uses was intended by Parliament to apply only to dwelling-houses.

Fifthly the use of any land for agriculture or forestry purposes (including buildings occupied with the land) does not constitute development. Two things should be said about this important exception to planning control which of course reflects the interest of planning legislation in the conservation of agricultural land. First it is only the use which is within the exception.

Operations over the land therefore require planning permission. (However the General Development Order 1977 grants
permission for many such operations: G.D.O. 1977 (No. 289),
Sched. I, Class VI). Secondly, it is questionable whether so
generous an exemption is justifiable.

Changes between different kinds of agricultural use, for
example, from market garden to battery chicken rearing, may
raise environmental issues which a planning authority should be
able to evaluate. Indeed some agricultural processes are more
akin to industrial activities and by exempting them from
planning controls the Act produces the risk that local authority
policy may be frustrated as regards the balance of uses within its
area. Moreover it is questionable whether forestry should be
assimilated with agriculture and exempted from control since
the practice of foresting unspoilt hill areas raises its own
environmental problems (for the meaning of "agriculture" see
section 290 (1) and *Belmont Farms Ltd.* v. *Minister of Housing*
(1962) 13 P. & C.R. 417).

Finally, acts which fall within classes of use specified by an
order made by the Secretary of State do not constitute
development. The order currently in force is the Use Classes
Order 1972 (No. 1385). This lists 18 classes of use. A change
within a class is not development. For example, Class I consists
of shops for any purpose with certain exceptions, comprising
shops which are potential nuisances (hot food shops, tripe shops
and motor vehicle shops are three such exceptions). Moreover
"shop" is defined to exclude other potentially unsavoury retail
activities, such as garages and launderettes. Thus a change from
a sweet shop to a shoe shop is not development. However a
change between classes or one from within a class to a use not
mentioned in the order at all is not *necessarily* development
either. The question depends upon the application of general
principles and in particular whether the change is "material."
Thus a change from a sweet shop to a launderette would

probably constitute development because of the environmental and traffic problems caused by launderettes, but a change between Class XVI use as a public hall and Class XVII use as a theatre would arguably not.

The classes are grouped upon the basis that the activities within a given class are roughly equivalent in terms of nuisance value. Thus Classes III–IX consist of seven categories of industrial building ranged in ascending order of offensiveness beginning with light industry (Class III). This consists of processes "such as could be carried on or installed in any residential area without detriment to the amenity of that area by reason of noise, vibration, smell, fumes, smoke, soot, ash, dust or grit." Thus difficult questions of fact may arise as to whether a particular proposal falls within the class. At the other end of the scale Class IX consists of listed industries which include bone grinding, blood boiling and breeding maggots from putrescible animal matter which although uncommon are indubitably offensive.

It is not proposed to discuss specific questions of construction of the order except to note that normal principles of statutory interpretation apply so that the court should not lean either in favour of or against bringing any particular use within its terms. (*Cf. Tessier* v. *Secretary of State* (1971) 69 L.G.R. 286.) The general criticism has been made of the Use Classes Order that it is inflexible. It excludes the specified changes of use from planning control even though local circumstances may vary. Thus there may be problems such as employment or traffic density caused by a change of use within a class. The planning authority will be unable to intervene, except under its general power to prohibit any use upon payment of compensation. Unlike the General Development Order 1977 (see below, pp. 77–78) which grants blanket planning permission in respect of prescribed categories of development, the Use Classes Order cannot be withdrawn or modified upon a selective basis.

Acts which are development

Section 22 (3), which is expressed to be "for the avoidance of doubt," defines two cases where development does take place. One is straightforward, that of the deposit of refuse on land. This is a material change of use even where the site is already used for the same purpose unless neither the surface area of the deposit is extended nor its height so as to exceed the level of the surrounding land. Thus infilling does not constitute development except in the case of a site not previously used as a rubbish dump (see *Ratcliffe* v. *Secretary of State for the Environment* (1975) 235 E.G. 901; *Alexandra Transport Ltd.* v. *Secretary of State for Scotland* (1973) 27 P. & C.R. 352).

The other case is more difficult. This is the use as two or more separate dwelling-houses of any building previously used as a single dwelling-house. The problem here is to establish what makes a separate dwelling-house (subs. (3) (*a*)). The phrase "separate dwellings" is also found in the Rent Acts, and has been defined in that context to mean a situation where there is no sharing of living accommodation, even though a toilet and bathroom may be shared (see *Neale* v. *Del Soto* [1945] K.B. 144; *Cole* v. *Harris* [1945] K.B. 474; *Goodrich* v. *Paisner* [1957] A.C. 65). It is doubtful whether the same test is appropriate in a planning context where the nature of the shared facilities seems irrelevant. It has been held that multiple occupation even by families living separately does not itself turn a single house into "separate dwellings" for planning purposes (*Ealing Corporation* v. *Ryan* [1965] 2 Q.B. 486; see also *Birmingham Corporation* v. *Habib Ullah* [1964] 1 Q.B. 178). In the *Ealing* case the Divisional Court found it unnecessary to hold whether the Rent Act test should apply in a planning context and indicated that further argument upon the scope of the planning legislation would be desirable, assisted by a representative of the Minister as *amicus curiae*.

However, in *Wakelin* v. *Secretary of State for the Environ-*

ment [1978] (*The Times*, June 11,) the Court of Appeal took the view that occupation by separate households is sufficient to attract subsection (3) (*a*) on the basis that this involves the creation of separate planning units. There a lodge was originally occupied by the staff of an adjoining dwelling-house. The owner now wished to lease the lodge for residence unconnected with the main house and this was held to be development. The planning authority could therefore intervene by permitting separate occupation only by persons related to the residents of the main house. Such a restriction was thought to serve the interests of privacy and its validity was not questioned.

It seems therefore that the *Ealing* and *Habib Ullah* cases are no longer good law, although they can be distinguished in that the relevant activities took place within a single building. Finally, section 23 (4) provides that the use of any external part of a building for the display of advertisements constitutes a material change of use where the part in question is not normally used for such purposes.

Notes

1 An application for planning permission is deemed also to be a section 53 application (*Wells* v. *Minister of Housing* [1967] 1 W.L.R. 1000). Apart from that a section 53 application must be in writing (*Western Fish Products Ltd.* v. *Penwith B.C.* [1978] J.P.L. 623). Is a person who receives planning permission thereby estopped from claiming later (*i.e.* in enforcement proceedings) that no permission is required because his activities do not constitute development? (*East Barnet U.D.C.* v. *B.T.C.* [1962] 2 Q.B. 484; *Newbury D.C.* v. *Secretary of State* (1979) 37 P. & C.R. 73).

2 Where the question is solely one of law then the landowner can apply directly to the courts. *Cf. Pyx Granite Co.* case (above). In all cases the local planning authority's decision can be challenged in the courts. There is no need first to appeal to the Secretary of State. *Cf. Marshall* v. *Nottingham Corporation* [1960] 1 W.L.R. 707.

3 See section 290 (1). Mining operations must for some purposes be treated as uses. See Town and Country Planning (Minerals) Regulations 1971 (No. 756); see also *Parkes* v. *Secretary of State for the Environment* [1978] *The Times*, May 10 (see below, p. 53).

4 *Cf. Re Windham's S.E.* [1912] 2 Ch. 75; *Re Walker's S.E.* [1894] 1 Ch. 189. To what extent is the analogy of these cases relevant in a planning context?

5 *E.g.*, the supply of accommodation, traffic, local services. See *Mayflower Cambridge Ltd.* v. *Secretary of State* (1975) 30 P. & C.R. 28.

6 Other cases involving identity are *Wakelin* v. *Secretary of State for the Environment* [1978] *The Times*, June 11, which turned upon the special provision in section 22 (3) (see below, pp. 70–71); *Clarke* v. *Minister of Housing* (1966) 18 P. & C.R. 82, which however can be explained on the ancillary use basis as perhaps can *Wilson* itself (see below, pp. 61–62).

7 It follows that the accidental destruction of a building by fire destroys its existing use rights. It is clear moreover that the demolition of a building raises no presumption in favour of granting permission for its rebuilding: *Magia Services* v. *Secretary of State for the Environment* [1978] J.P.L. 383. *Gray* v. *Minister of Housing* (1964) 68 L.G.R. 15 however can be read as supporting the contrary proposition, since the case turned upon whether use rights had been established prior to destruction by fire. However, this was prior to *Petticoat Lane Rentals*.

8 However the case was also treated as one of intensification of the unit as a whole (including both the building and the surrounding land). The Court of Appeal held that there was no evidence of such intensification. See (1979) 37 P. & C.R. 129. The Petticoat Lane Rentals point was not discussed in the Court of Appeal.

Chapter 3

APPLICATIONS FOR PLANNING PERMISSION

Once it has been established that a proposed activity constitutes development it then has to be decided whether an application must be made for planning permission. Even if this is the case the developer may prefer to carry out his development without permission (bearing in mind that no penalty is attached to this in itself), and to wait for the authority to take enforcement action. This it may never do. Even if it does the developer can appeal to the Secretary of State against the enforcement notice. The appeal suspends the operation of the notice (section 88 (3)) and is also deemed to be an application for planning permission (section 88 (7)). By taking this provocative course of action the developer risks a small fine, but more seriously may be required to dismantle any buildings which he has erected without permission. Whether the risk is worth taking depends partly upon economic factors, bearing in mind that several years may elapse between commencing the unauthorised development and being required to cease. A retail outlet located in an existing building may be a more worthwhile risk than the extension of a factory.

In the following three classes of cases there is no need to apply for planning permission. Moreover except in special cases the Act does not apply to land held by the Crown (see Appendix).

1. *Exemption from the Need for Planning Permission*

First, section 23 provides for six situations where no planning permission is needed. All concern cases of reversion to previous uses of land. Three are of limited importance and concern transitional situations where a landowner was prejudiced by the introduction of planning controls in 1947.[1]

The other three are of greater significance. They illustrate the proposition that it is a change of use and not a use itself which requires planning permission. Thus exemptions are given in respect of the return to the "normal" use of land after the expiry of a temporary planning permission and of a limited permission granted by development order. The "normal" use is that existing before the grant of permission. It does not include any use begun in breach of planning control. (Section 23 (5) (*b*).)

This exemption is more difficult. It deals with the situation where a landowner is obeying an enforcement notice and allows him to use his land "for the purpose for which it could . . . *lawfully* have been used," if the development forbidden by the notice had not been carried out (section 23 (9)). The subsection is badly drafted. There is, first, no definition of "lawful" whereas in the other two cases uses begun in breach of control are not allowed. Secondly, it is inapt to refer to a "lawful use" of land. It is the act of change which constitutes development and not the use itself.

The main problem arises because there is no sanction attached to development without permission. It can therefore be argued that nothing is unlawful until it has actually been prohibited by an enforcement notice. This however would defeat the entire system of development control. A landowner who wishes to use his land as, say, a secondhand car salesroom but knows that permission would not be granted could first use the land for something else making sure that this is sufficiently repulsive to attract enforcement proceedings. Upon service of the enforcement notice he could then switch to the car sales use claiming the benefit of section 23 (9) which does not expressly stipulate that the lawful use must have previously existed.

A narrower meaning must therefore be given to "lawful." In *LTSS Print & Supply Co.* v. *Hackney B.C.* [1976] Q.B. 663 the Court of Appeal held that a use is "unlawful" even if it is immune from enforcement proceedings because of the time limits for serving an enforcement notice. (Uses begun before 1963 are so immune.) This means that, despite the time limit, conveyancers will often have to investigate the planning history of a site back to 1948. The *Hackney* case has been criticised upon the assumption that conveyancing convenience is a paramount consideration. From both a logical and a planning point of view the decision is perfectly acceptable. (Compare the curious Divisional Court decision in *Lamb* v. *Secretary of State* [1975] 2 All E.R. 1117.)

First, a procedural bar such as a time limit does not legalise an act which was unlawful in its inception: *R.* v. *Governor of Pentonville Prison, ex p. Azam* [1974] A.C. 18. The sanctionless duty can have indirect practical consequences (see *Seymour* v. *Pickett* [1905] 1 K.B. 715; *Britain* v. *Rossiter* (1879) 11 Q.B.D. 123).

Secondly, the reason for making pre-1964 uses immune from enforcement is to prevent long-established arrangements being upset. This has no application in the present context, since the old use no longer exists. The pre-1964 use has been extinguished by the implementation of the use against which the enforcement notice issues and there is no reason why the landowner should be entitled to reactivate it (see above, p. 60). Indeed if section 23 (9) applied to pre-1964 uses a person who made an illegal change of use and was visited by an enforcement notice would be in a better position than once who changed with planning permission since in the latter case there can be no return to previous use without a further permission (apart from the special cases mentioned above).

D

A "lawful" use is therefore a use which was instituted lawfully, *i.e.* either with planning permission or not requiring planning permission. This ensures that the landowner served with an enforcement notice changes to an activity which is acceptable from a planning point of view. Not every lawful use is within the exemption, which refers only to uses which would have been lawful *had the development forbidden by the notice not taken place*. Thus where land is used with planning permission for, say, car sales, and then is used for storage purposes without permission, and finally for manufacturing in respect of which an enforcement notice is served, there is no "lawful" use within the exemption, because the car sales use was lost when the "unlawful" storage use was implemented.

2. *Permission by Development Order*

The second situation where no application for planning permission is needed is quite different. Here planning permission is granted by a development order. This is a statutory instrument made by the Secretary of State subject to parliamentary approval (section 24). Development orders can either grant planning permission or specify requirements for applications for permission. They can either be special or general. A special development order grants permission in respect either of a specific development or of a prescribed area of land. It can be used for example where a proposal raises political issues which deserve parliamentary debate. Thus proposals in respect of the third London airport and more recently in connection with the application to extend the Windscale nuclear processing establishment were dealt with by special development orders (*cf.* S.I. 1978 No. 523). Looked at from a more sinister point of view development order procedure avoids the obligation to hold a public inquiry which would arise where there is an appeal against the refusal of an express planning permission (*cf. Essex C.C.* v. *Ministry of Housing* (1967) 18 P. & C.R. 531).

A general development order (of which the current example is the General Development Order 1977 (No. 289) (herein-after called the GDO) grants blanket planning permission for the activities listed in Schedule 1. It is intended to avoid the need to make specific applications in uncontroversial cases and is a useful device by which central government can regulate the exercise of power by local planning authorities. Permission is given for 23 classes of development. Particulars of these are given in the standard textbooks and they will not be discussed in detail here. Most are minor activities. Thus Class I authorises the enlargement, improvement or other alteration of dwelling-houses subject to precise requirements as to size (see *Bradford M.D.C.* v. *Secretary of State* (1978) 245 E.G. 573). Some of the classes concern development by statutory authorities. (See Appendix.)

Class IV is of general importance and permits the use of land, but not of buildings, for up to 28 days in any calendar year. This has caused difficulty where the use has continued after 28 days, sometimes on a permanent basis. For the purpose of defining the offence and for other purposes such as time limits, it seems that the entire use is unlawfully instituted and not just the excess over 28 days. Thus the GDO permission can be taken advantage of only where the use in fact lasts 28 days or less (see *Miller-Mead* v. *Minister of Housing* [1963] 2 Q.B. 196; see below, p. 146n.). Even where the use has continued for less than 28 days it may be that evidence that the use is intended to be temporary is needed to invoke the protection of the GDO (*cf. Tidswell* v. *Secretary of State for the Environment* (1976) 34 P. & C.R. 152). It is also uncertain whether the 28 days' permission can be exercised in addition to any other temporary rights in respect of the same use. The point was left open in *Postill* v. *East Riding C.C.* [1956] 2 Q.B. 386 where there was also a "normal use" exemption for a few days each year. It is suggested that the exemption is intended to operate only for a maximum of 28 days and that any other use rights must be offset against the period. In any event the suggestion made by early commentators that all changes of use are authorised by the GDO for an initial period of 28 days is clearly wrong (see [1960] J.P.L. 531).

Under article 4 the Secretary of State or the local planning authority[2] may withdraw the benefit of any GDO permission either generally or in relation to a particular piece of land. This means that the landowner will need to make an application for planning permission. If permission is then refused compensation is payable (see section 165 (2)). This power is a useful device for retaining stringent controls in special cases (see *e.g.* *Thanet D.C.* v. *Ninedrive Ltd.* [1978] 1 All E.R. 703).

An article 4 direction just like any other revocation of permission cannot be made once the development in question has been implemented: *Cole* v. *Somerset C.C.* [1957] 1 Q.B. 23.[3]

It is sometimes suggested that the GDO should be more liberal and include within its ambit a larger number of small acts of development. This would reduce the workload of local planning authorities. However Dobry rejected this upon the basis that a general relaxation would be objectionable on environmental grounds. For example, the extension of a rural cottage might in isolation be insignificant but the cumulative effect of many such extensions could have a disastrous effect upon the appearance of a locality. Nevertheless specific relaxations of parts of the order were recommended (Dobry, pp. 100–105), but have not been implemented.[4]

3. *Deemed Planning Permission*

Finally there are a few special cases where planning permission is "deemed to be granted." These mainly involve development by public authorities and will be outlined in the Appendix.[5]

Application Procedure

Any person can apply for planning permission in respect of any piece of land. For example, a prospective purchaser as well as the landowner himself may make an application. It is not unknown for third parties to apply for planning permission merely in order to delay a decision upon an objectionable application made by the landowner himself since all proposals have to be considered by the authority.

However, to avoid injustices and particularly financial loss which could arise if the owner of the land were unaware of an application (*cf. Hanily* v. *Minister of Housing* [1952] 2 Q.B. 444) section 27 provides that every application for planning permission must be accompanied by a certificate which states either that 21 days before the date of the application no one other than the applicant was the owner of the land or that all owners have been given notice of the application. Should the applicant be unable to issue this certificate he must provide another one stating that he has taken reasonable steps to ascertain the names and addresses of the persons concerned. A similar requirement exists for the service of notice upon tenants of agricultural holdings (section 27 (3)). An owner is defined for this purpose by reference to the concept of a "material interest" in section 6 of the Community Land Act 1975 and means a freehold owner or the owner of a lease, the unexpired term of which is at least seven years. Thus holders of short leases and indeed the occupiers of the land, for example beneficiaries under a trust, do not have to be notified. However, a major difficulty in English land law with its tradition of secret conveyancing is that it is sometimes difficult to find out who owns a given piece of land (*cf.* Dowrick [1974] P.L. 10 particularly note 2).

In *R.* v. *Bradford-on-Avon U.D.C., ex p. Boulton* [1964] 1 W.L.R. 1136 it was held that a planning permission is valid even if granted on the strength of a factually incorrect certificate. The applicant mistakenly assumed that he was the owner of the land in question but part of it was vested in someone else. There was therefore no element of fraud which would have invalidated the certificate. The decision can be justified upon the basis that it is important for conveyancing purposes that third parties should be able to take such documents at their face value. It is also consistent with the basic principle of administrative law that error of fact does not invalidate a decision.

However the *Bradford-on-Avon* case does militate against one of the purposes of section 27 since a landowner who is not informed of an application may well sell his land for less than its market value.

It may be that private law can provide a remedy. This is certainly the case where the applicant expressly holds himself out to be the agent of the landowner. Here even if there was no existing fiduciary relationship and even if the landowner is unaware of the applicant's conduct it has been held that the applicant is under a fiduciary duty to account for his profits (*i.e.* the development value) to the owner (see *England* v. *Dedham Vale Property Co.* [1978] 1 W.L.R. 93). The applicant will be a constructive trustee of the development value for the landowner. It may be that even without an actual holding out the *England* case can support a wide principle based upon unjust enrichment (see note in (1978) 94 L.Q.R. 347).

Could an action in tort lie against an applicant who fails to notify the landowner? It is clear that an action in contract would not succeed unless there had been a misrepresentation. The vendor who sells cheap to a purchaser who has received planning permission cannot rescind for mistake any more than one who sells without knowing that his purchaser has arranged to sell at a higher price to someone else.

However it is arguable that section 27 gives rise to a duty of care on the part of the applicant towards the landowner. It is not a statutory duty since the statutory obligation is merely to forward a certificate and is owed to the authority, but a common law duty to take reasonable care in making statements on the certificate. It is clear from *Ministry of Housing* v. *Sharp* [1970] 2 Q.B. 223, which concerned a negligent failure to register a land charge, that there can be liability towards persons who incur foreseeable loss as a result of an erroneous or incomplete statement to a third party. It is reasonably foreseeable that a landowner may incur loss if he is not told of the application, and it is clear that a sale of property at less than its market value can give rise to an action for damages (*Arenson* v. *Casson* [1975] 3 W.L.R. 815). The question whether a duty of care should be imposed in novel situations depends first upon reasonable foreseeability. Once this test is satisfied there is a presumption in favour of the imposition of a duty which can be rebutted by policy considerations. There is, it is submitted, no reason why the applicant who negligently furnishes an incorrect certificate should not be liable.

The detailed procedure for applying for planning permission is governed by the GDO. This provides for application forms accompanied by detailed plans of the proposed development and such other information as the authority requires. The application must be submitted to the district planning authority which either decides the case itself or, where a county matter (see p. 119) is involved, forwards it to the county council. In addition the Secretary of State can "call in" any application to decide himself (section 35). Where the Secretary of State decides an application he must, unlike the local authority, hold an inquiry into objections, thus in some cases giving the public an opportunity to comment on the proposal (see Chap. 8). The Secretary of State may also give directions restricting grants of planning permission (section 31 (1)).

The question arises as to whether the local planning authority must give any person a hearing before deciding an application.

The GDO requires consultation with other public authorities affected by the proposal including, if they so request, parish councils (arts. 15–19). There is also provision in certain cases for public notice to be given and objections invited and considered (s. 26; s. 29 (2)). [6] These cases are listed in the GDO, art. 8 and are commonly called "bad neighbour" development. The list is a limited one including such developments as public conveniences, knackers yards, zoos, theatres and cemetaries and consists essentially of small-scale developments which although capable of being offensive are of limited economic importance. It appears to be government policy to treat the duty to publicise applications as a limited and exceptional one. In practice, however, many authorities publicise most applications and invite objections, (see Dobry, pp. 39–40). In the bad neighbour cases the applicant is required both to post a notice on the land in question and to publish a notice in the local newspaper (section 26). The authority may not then consider an application unless it is accompanied by a certificate stating either that these requirements have been met or that the applicant has been unable to post the site notice because of difficulties as to rights of access.

Provision for notice and advertisement is also made in the case of certain applications within conservation areas (section 28).

Finally, applications which in the authority's opinion conflict with the development plan must, unless the authority proposes to refuse permission, also be advertised and objections invited (Town and Country Planning (Development Plans) Direction 1975; see Circular 96/75; see also p. 20, above). In these last two cases the duty to advertise is imposed upon the authority and not the applicant.[6]

There is thus no general statutory right to a hearing. Indeed the Government has rejected the Dobry proposal that publicity should be compulsory in all cases and favours the present system of leaving publicity largely to the discretion of the authority itself (see Circular 113/75). Can it therefore be argued that the common law rules of natural justice require that the applicant and third parties be afforded a hearing? It must be borne in mind in this connection that there are approximately 450,000 applications for planning permission each year. Before 1964 the law was restrictive but clear. The right to be heard applied only to a judicial decision. Although the meaning of "judicial" is by no means clear (see below, pp. 167–168), it is reasonably certain that a planning permission is to be classified as an administrative rather than as a judicial decision (*R.* v. *Hillingdon B.C., ex p. Royco Homes Ltd.* [1974] Q.B. 720). A planning permission lacks two important indicia associated with judicial decisions. First, the decision is one of policy rather than of the application of fixed rules of law. Secondly, a planning permission can be classified as a privilege and thus refusal of permission cannot be said to deprive the applicant of any right (*cf. Westminster Bank* v. *Minister of Housing* [1971] A.C. 508).

However, since the leading case of *Ridge* v. *Baldwin* [1964] A.C. 40, it has been established that even administrative decisions attract an obligation to act "fairly" (see *e.g. Re Pergamon Press* [1971] Ch. 388; *Re H.K.* [1967] 2 Q.B. 617) and that fairness may require that an applicant for a licence or privilege be heard (*R.* v. *Gaming Board for Great Britain, ex p. Benaim and Khaida* [1970] 2 Q.B. 417). Indeed in one case the Court of Appeal held that third parties, members of a taxi operators' association, were entitled to be heard before a local authority changed its policy in respect of the grant of additional taxi licences (*R.* v. *Liverpool Corporation* [1972] 2 Q.B. 299). Lord Denning M.R. based his reasoning upon the impact of the policy upon the applicants' economic interests. It follows from this that a similar right to be heard should apply to planning permissions. However, the other members of the court relied upon a previous undertaking specifically given by the council that the applicants would be consulted.

In one pre-1947 case it was held that the bias rule of natural justice applied to a planning permission (*R.* v. *Hendon U.D.C., ex p. Chorley* [1933] 2 K.B. 696). It does not necessarily follow however that there is also a right to be heard. Moreover the limited form of land use control which existed before 1947 made it easier to argue that planning permissions were judicial in character and affected "rights" (but see *Hanily* v. *Minister of Local Government* [1952] 2 Q.B. 444, 452).

The question to be asked today is whether it would be unfair not to afford the applicant a hearing. It is suggested that an applicant for planning permission has in principle a right to be heard because of the impact of a refusal upon his interests. However, the requirements of a fair hearing are minimal. The courts have extended the *scope* of natural justice to embrace licensing, but have taken a more restrictive attitude to its *content*. There are no fixed requirements of a hearing and the actual procedure is a matter for the discretion of the authority. Administrative convenience and the need to minimise delay are relevant factors (see *Local Government Board* v. *Arlidge* [1915] A.C. 120). Thus natural justice does not necessarily entail an oral hearing, nor cross-examination, nor disclosure of documents. All that is required is that the applicant know in substance the case against him and be given a chance to state his views. Indeed the procedures which planning authorities normally use seem to satisfy these requirements. The application form (see Dobry, pp. 168–169) allows information to be submitted in relation to the land itself and the applicant may be interviewed by a council official, but in any event can submit a personal statement by letter. An official will normally make a site visit and there will be informal consultation between council and applicant. (See McLoughlin, *Control and Urban Planning*, Chap. 4). It is suggested that an application to the court based upon breach of natural justice would be possible only in the event of an arbitrary refusal by the authority to consult with the applicant. Thus in *R.* v. *Sheffield Corp.* (1979) 37 P. & C.R. 1, it was held that there was no obligation formally to consult with the occupants of a caravan site in respect of which an application was made, as long as the authority took their views into account.

It is clear that third parties such as neighbours have no general right to be heard. Even if the wide *ratio* of Lord Denning M.R. in the *Liverpool Corporation* case (above) is relied upon, there is an established principle that a statutory provision for a hearing in specific circumstances must be taken to indicate that there is to be no hearing in other cases (*Pearlberg* v. *Varty* [1972] 1 W.L.R. 534, *Bates* v. *Lord Hailsham* [1972] 1 W.L.R. 1373. Thus the specific provisions in sections 26 and 28 may exclude any general right to be heard. It may be, however, that a person who shows that an application bears particularly hard upon him so as, for example, to interfere with his amenities or to reduce the value of his property would have a right to a hearing to the extent of requiring the authority to consider a written representation. In this connection is has been held that a planning authority is obliged to take into account the impact of a development upon the private rights of neighbours and this minimal right to be heard may follow from this (*Stringer* v. *Minister of Housing* [1970] 1 W.L.R. 1281).

Even if there is no legal right to a hearing it may be possible to show that a failure to consult neighbours in respect of an application which adversely affects them constitutes "maladministration" within the jurisdiction of the local Ombudsman (*cf.* [1978] J.P.L. 120).

Outline Planning Permission

Where planning permission is required for the erection of a building the GDO provides a simplified procedure whereby the applicant can obtain permission in principle subject to the subsequent approval by the authority of detailed matters. When application is made for outline permission detailed plans do not have to be provided and permission is granted subject to a condition that a later application (which is subject to a simplified procedure (art. 6)) be made for the approval of "reserved matters." These are defined in article 2 (1) as matters of siting, design, external appearance, means of access and landscaping.

There is no reason why, in the case of any planning permission, an authority should not grant a conditional permission subject to the approval of further details. However, except in cases governed by the outline application procedure a detailed application including plans must be made. The outline procedure thus saves expense and delay. Moreover under the outline procedure an appeal to the Secretary of State may be made in respect of a refusal to approve details. In other cases the appeal must be against the initial condition and may therefore be time-barred.

An outline planning permission is not an inchoate permission which becomes effective only upon the approval of reserved matters. It is full planning permission subject to a condition that it will lapse if the reserved matters are not approved within the specified time limit. Reserved matters must, unless the authority specifies otherwise, be submitted for approval within three years (section 42 (2)). Additionally, an express condition is often attached that the permission is to lapse unless the applicant is notified within a time limit that they have been approved. The House of Lords has upheld the validity of such a condition (*Kent C.C.* v. *Kingsway Investments* [1971] A.C. 72). The risk that the applicant may lose his permission because of delays outside his control is avoided by the provision that a decision upon a planning permission must be made within eight weeks (art. 7 (6)), in default of which the applicant can appeal to the Secretary of State (section 36). Moreover, even if the appeal decision is outside the time limit this will not cause the permission to lapse. Their Lordships construed the condition as including a case where the Secretary of State on appeal holds that the reserved matters *should* have been approved within the time limit. Thus as long as the applicant submits his details in good time the clock is effectively stopped.

The consequences of the outline permission being in itself an effective planning permission are important.

First, approval cannot be refused (except like any planning permission upon payment of compensation (section 45)) upon any grounds except those concerned with the reserved matters (*Hamilton* v. *West Sussex C.C.* [1958] 2 Q.B. 286; *Chelmsford Corp.* v. *Secretary of State* (1971) 22 P. & C.R. 880). The authority thus cannot have second thoughts. It is not certain whether, when the authority considers the reserved matters, it can attach further conditions to its approval (*Chelmsford Corp.* v. *Secretary of State*, above, at pp. 987–988). It is suggested that no such conditions can be attached. An authority can only attach conditions to a planning permission. The planning permission is the initial outline permission and all conditions must be attached at that stage. Approval of the reserved matters is not in itself a planning permission and therefore no conditions can be attached, even if the authority purported to reserve the right to do so when it granted outline permission.

Secondly, the authority must be taken impliedly to approve all matters contained in the initial application except those which it expressly reserves for subsequent approval. In this connection difficulties of construction may arise. In the first place the outline application may in itself include detailed plans relating, for example, to the proposed layout of the development. Unless it is made clear that these are merely illustrative they will form part of the permission and both authority and developer will be bound.

Moreover, an application for approval of details may differ so greatly from the original application as to constitute a fresh application for planning permission. If this is the case then the matter can be considered *ab initio* and permission refused on principle. (*Shemara* v. *Luton Corporation* (1967) 18 P. & C.R. 520). This will not in itself affect the earlier outline permission because a planning permission is not lost merely because an inconsistent permission is subsequently sought (see below, pp. 113–117). As long as there is time left, a fresh application for approval of reserved matters can be made. If on the other hand the differences between the outline permission and the subsequent application are trivial the case will be treated merely as an application for approval of reserved matters. In this context it was suggested in *Hamilton* (above) that if an authority refused an application for reasons irrelevant to the reserved matters, then the reserved matters must be taken impliedly to be approved. This has subsequently been doubted (*Shemara*, above) and the correct view seems to be that the second decision is a nullity so that a fresh application must be made for approval of details. However, in *Cardiff Corporation* v. *Secretary of State for Wales* (1971) 22 P. & C.R. 718 Thesiger J. held that an application can be at the same time a fresh application *and*, if it contains appropriate information, an application for approval of reserved matters. It is thus open to the authority to reject the fresh application but expressly to approve the reserved matters.[7]

Finally, a refusal to approve the reserved matters does not itself terminate an outline permission. There can be repeated applications for approval in relation to the whole or part of the land even where approval has already been given and the developer wishes to change his mind as to the details of his development (*cf. R.* v. *Secretary of State for the Environment, ex p. Percy Bilton* (1975) 31 P. & C.R. 154; *Heron Corporation* v. *Manchester City Council* [1978] 1 W.L.R. 937. The permission

will expire if details are not approved by the end of the time
limit.

Notes

1 See Heap, p. 84 and *Kingdom* v. *Minister of Housing* [1968] 1 Q.B. 257.

2 With the approval of the Secretary of State except in certain cases when the
local authority can withdraw the order for up to six months (art. 43).

3 *Quaere* whether this means the commencement or the completion of
operational development. A change of use is a single act notionally
instantaneous. It is suggested that commencement of the operation prevents
revocation by analogy with the general principle of estoppel.

4 See [1978] J.P.L. 2 and 30.

5 See also section 64 and Sched. 24, para. 1 (3).

6 A failure to advertise probably invalidates the permission. See de Smith,
pp. 124–125. But compare the drafting of sections 26, 27 and 28.

7 *Langley* v. *Warwick D.C.* (1975) 73 L.G.R. 171 postulated another possibility that of "an agreed variation." See also Dobry, pp. 76–78.

Chapter 4

THE DISCRETION OF THE AUTHORITY

General Considerations

Planning permission may be granted unconditionally or subject to such conditions as the authority thinks fit (section 29 (1)). There are few statutory limits upon this power apart from procedural ones. The Act requires authorities to have regard to the provisions of the development plan and to any other material considerations but without specifying what these are.[1] The Secretary of State gives guidance to local planning authorities on matters of relevance and policy by means of appeal decisions and circulars (see *e.g.* Circular 51/68) but these are not binding on the courts. Indeed a local planning authority which fetters its individual direction by treating itself as bound by the Secretary of State is acting unlawfully as is the Secretary of State himself if he accepts instructions from another government department[2] (see *Lavender* v. *Minister of Housing* [1970] 1 W.L.R. 1231). In practice ministerial decisions and circulars are given considerable weight and the rule against fettering discretion may effectively be no more than a formal one (see below, p. 101). The basic concern of this branch of the law is to determine where the line between the spheres of influence of court and executive should be drawn. Phrases like "unreasonableness" are not in themselves helpful except in as much as they emphasise that judicial review is reserved for

exceptional cases, and that English judges avoid pronounce-
ments upon policy matters. It is in the area of procedure that the
courts show themselves at their most interventionist having in
recent years developed the rules of natural justice into a general
requirement of "acting fairly." Even here however, the need to
preserve executive discretion has exercised considerable
influence so that the duty to act fairly entails few if any absolute
procedural requirements (see Wade, pp. 451–468).

In the area of substantive limits upon discretion the courts
have been less willing to intervene and there are few cases of
where the citizen has been successful.

The grounds upon which a decision can be challenged in the
courts have been formulated in several different ways.
Inconsistent terminology is one of the bugbears of this subject
and there is little agreement as to how to classify the various
grounds of judicial review.[3] Both the Scilla of over-
simplification and the Charybdis of using differing language to
mean the same thing need particular attention (see *e.g. Hanks*
v. *Minister of Housing* [1963] 1 Q.B. 999, 1020; *Associated
Provincial Picture Houses* v. *Wednesbury Corporation* [1948] 1
K.B. 223, 228–229; *Western Fish Products* v. *Penwith B.C.*
[1978] J.P.L. 623).

The following classification is suggested:

A discretionay decision can be challenged first if it violates an
express statutory requirement whether substantive or procedural (see below, p. 113 n. for the effect of breach of procedural requirements); secondly, if it violates the rules of natural
justice where applicable; thirdly, if irrelevant considerations
are taken into account or relevant considerations not taken into
account, and fourthly, if it is unreasonable. In all these cases the
authority is regarded as having exceeded or failed to exercise its
statutory powers so that its decision is a nullity.[4]

The notion that an *ultra vires* decision is void raises a problem
where the decision is partly invalid. Can the bad be severed

from the good or does the whole decision fall? The question arises in connection with conditions attached to a planning permission. Thus a person who successfully challenges a condition will lose the whole planning permission unless the condition can be severed. The law is extremely uncertain. Only Winn L.J. dissenting on the point in *Hall & Co.* v. *Shoreham U.D.C.* [1964] 1 W.L.R. 240 was prepared to apply the notion of nullity to the extent of holding that a void condition never affects the validity of the permission. At the other extreme it has been stated *obiter* that a planning permission and its conditions are so intimately related that a condition can never be severed (see *Pyx Granite Co.* v. *Ministry of Housing* [1958] 1 Q.B. 554, *per* Hodson L.J. and see Lord Guest in *Kent C.C.* v. *Kingsway Investments* [1971] AC 72, 107).

However the weight of authority supports a compromise based upon the importance of the condition in relation to the particular planning permission (*Hall & Co.* v. *Shoreham U.D.C.* (above), *R.* v. *Hillingdon B.C., ex p. Royco Homes Ltd* [1974] Q.B. 720).

In *Kent C.C.* v. *Kingsway Investments Ltd*. [1971] A.C. 72 their Lordships expressed a variety of views on the question of severance. A majority held that the matter depended upon the importance of the condition (Lords Morris, Upjohn and Donovan), but a different majority (Lords Morris, Guest, and Donovan) decided that the condition was valid anyway. No precise guidelines were laid down as to how to identify important conditions. Their Lordships employed such phrases as "affect the character of permission," and being "part of the structure of the permission" which do not take the matter any further. It was also suggested, by Lord Upjohn, that the correct approach was to ask whether the authority would have granted permission had they been aware that their condition would be illegal. This leans rather too much in favour of the authority. Indeed the majority who supported the importance test failed to agree upon its application to the particular circumstances. Lord Upjohn favoured severance but Lords Morris and Donovan would not have done.

Lord Reid attempted to supply a more specific test (at pp. 90–91). He distinguished three classes of condition. First, those imposed for reasons entirely unrelated to planning. These should always be severable; secondly, those imposed for proper planning reasons but invalid on the ground of unreasonableness—for example, an excessively harsh condition (see below, p. 102). These should not be severable if they relate to the way in which the development is carried out since unlike the first case the authority might have been able to refuse permission for the same reasons. They should not therefore be required to tolerate an activity which they did not intend to permit. The third category consists of conditions which are unreasonable but which do not affect the way in which the development is carried out. Severance of these depends upon the importance test.

Lord Reid's approach is attractive in that it is reasonably precise and consistent with the result (but not the dicta) in all the cases, in some of which severance was allowed without discussion (*Hartnell* v. *Minister of Housing* [1965] A.C. 1134; *Mixnam's Properties* v. *Chertsey U.D.C.* [1965] A.C. 735; *cf. Allnatt London Properties* v. *Middlesex C.C.* (1964) 15 P. & C.R. 288; *Hall and Royco* cases above).

However it is suggested that on principle the opinion of Winn L.J. to the effect that a condition can always be severed is preferable. Lord Reid's approach is complex and the distinction between conditions which affect the carrying out of the development and others is not altogether clear. Nor does it necessarily reflect any important policy distinction.

Moreover cases where severance is not permitted weigh the scales in favour of the authority which seems to be able to profit from its own wrong. It is not merely that the landowner is forced to choose between accepting an unreasonable condition or losing his permission, although this is certainly the case. The authority too would be able to rely upon the fact that its permission is void and serve an enforcement notice even if the conditions were complied with. Moreover even if neither principal party took action a third party such as a neighbour would be able to apply for certiorari to quash the planning permission. Where a decision is *ultra vires* it seems that it cannot be cured by doctrines such as consent or estoppel which might be invoked to deal with these kinds of problems.[5] If the authority regrets its grant of permission it can always revoke it as long as it pays compensation (sections 45 and 51).

Taking Irrelevant Factors Into Account

There have been few cases where the courts have held any factor actually to be irrelevant to planning. Such general indications as are to be found in the Act, particularly in connection with the obligation to prepare development plans, suggest that planning can legitimately be concerned with any aspect of the public interest (see above, p. 35). Attempts have been made to find a general limiting formula but these have proved largely unacceptable. Thus in *Stringer* v. *Minister of Housing* [1970] 1 W.L.R. 1281 Cooke J. refused first to limit the scope of planning to amenity matters, and secondly, to accept the proposition that planning should not concern itself with protecting the interests of individual landowners. These are an aspect of the public interest, and have to be balanced against the interests of third parties. His Lordship would treat all considerations relating to land use and development as, in principle, relevant.

Attempts have been made to contrast "planning" considerations with "housing or public health or social considerations other than town planning" (see Pearce L.J. in *Fawcett Properties Ltd* v. *Bucks C.C.* [1959] Ch. 543, 578).

This approach is based upon a misconception as to the function of the word "planning." Unlike such terms as "housing" it does not refer to any specific subject-matter but is a method. Planning is the technique of making arrangements for the future and can relate to any area of activity. It is a method of achieving objectives, and carries no implication as to what these objectives should be. Use of nebulous terms like "the public interest" have been criticised but is it desirable to be any more precise? Should it not rather be for the elected local authorities to decide what the "public interest" includes and to base judicial intervention not upon the controversial notion of relevance, but upon the doctrine of reasonableness?

The problem of controlling discretions concerns not only what controls should exist, but also who should impose controls and it is arguable that the courts are not well-equipped to determine questions of relevance in relation to social legislation. It is even worse to suggest that some *a priori* economic theory should provide a legal touchstone.

A plausible attempt to provide a general test has been made by those who argue that planning powers should not be used to duplicate powers available under other legislation, such as public health or housing (see Maxwell, *Interpretation of Statutes* (12th ed.), p. 196; see also MHLG Development Control Policy Note I). This is based upon the assumption that Parliament could not when passing the 1947 Act have intended a duplication of powers. There is, however, no support in the cases for this approach. Thus in *Westminster Bank* v. *Minister of Housing* [1971] A.C. 508 the House of Lords held that planning permission could be refused for the extension of the bank's premises in order to facilitate the council's road widening scheme even though an alternative way of preventing the development was available under the Highways Act 1959 and even though the alternative required compensation to be paid to the landowner. It was held not only that the Highways

Act power does not inhibit the exercise of planning powers but also that it is legitimate for the authority to choose between alternative powers upon the basis of cost and thus to select the method that requires no compensation (see also *Hoveringham Gravels* v. *Secretary of State* [1975] Q.B. 754). Safety, clean air, noise, health, and archaeological sites, are each regulated by other legislation but have nevertheless been held to be legitimate planning considerations (see *Fitzpatrick Developments* v. *Minister of Housing* (1965) 194 E.G. 911; *Esdell Caravan Parks* v. *Hemel Hempstead R.D.C.* [1966] 1 Q.B. 895, 925; *R.M.C. Management Services* v. *Secretary of State* (1972) 222 E.G. 1593.

Their Lordships left open the possibility that in exceptional cases a choice cannot be made where, for example, the other procedure is the more normal one. This suggests an approach based upon reasonableness rather than relevance.

There have been several miscellaneous cases which lend support to the proposition that the courts are unwilling to stigmatise a consideration as irrelevant unless it is clearly unreasonable. Thus in *Clyde & Co. Ltd.* v. *Secretary of State* [1977] 1 W.L.R. 926 the Court of Appeal held that permission could be refused solely upon the basis that it was desirable to preserve the existing use, which in that case was residential at a time of housing shortage (*cf. Granada Theatres Ltd.* v. *Secretary of State* [1976] J.P.L. 96). An authority can also use the "floodgates" principle and refuse permission for fear of inciting large numbers of similar applications. (*Collis Radio Ltd.* v. *Secretary of State* (1975) 29 P. & C.R. 390).

In one respect, however, the notion of relevance is significant. This is in the case of conditions (which can be attached not only to the land subject to the permission but also to other land under the control of the applicant (section 30 (1) (*a*))[5a] It is clear that a condition must be relevant to the development which forms the subject-matter of the application

(*Pyx Granite Co.* v. *Ministry of Housing* [1958] 1 Q.B. 554). This means that the condition must have a physical effect upon the development. Thus if permission was granted for the extension to a factory on condition that another factory in another part of the town be knocked down then the condition would be void for irrelevance even though the motive for its imposition was both a proper planning one and concerned the new development. Conversely, permission was granted for the working of a quarry subject to a valid condition limiting the use of an adjacent processing plant (*Pyx Granite* case, above). The two pieces of land were used in conjunction and the level of use of the processing plant would affect that of the quarry (see also *A.I. & P. (Stratford) Ltd.* v. *London Borough of Tower Hamlets* [1976] J.P.L. 234, and *Penwith D.C.* v. *Secretary of State for the Environment* [1977] J.P.L. 371).

However, in *Newbury D.C.* v. *Secretary of State for the Environment* [1978] 1 All E.R. 243, the Court of Appeal took a broader approach. A temporary permission was granted to store rubber goods in an old aircraft hangar. A condition requiring the demolition of the hangar at the end of the permission was upheld by the Court of Appeal. Lord Denning M.R. thought that his judgment in the *Pyx Granite* case had been taken too narrowly. However, apart from asserting that the condition was related to the development their Lordships gave no explanation of their reasoning. The permitted development was a change of use. It is difficult to see how the demolition of the building which existed long before permission was granted has any relationship to the use as opposed to the land on which the use was carried out. The position of buildings constructed under the permission for purposes connected with it is entirely different and the Act specifically provides that conditions can require these to be demolished (section 30 (1) (*b*)).

Their Lordships were influenced by the fact that the only other means of ensuring the removal of the unsightly hangar involved the authority having to pay compensation. This case shows the court being far from sympathetic towards private property rights. The scope of Lord Denning M.R.'s proposition is moreover extremely vague. Could an authority, for example, give permission for the conversion of a dwelling-house temporarily into flats and attach a condition that the house be demolished at the end of the period?

A condition is also valid which requires other land to be put to a specific use, as long as the use is ancillary to that which forms the subject of the application (*Hitchens* v. *Secretary of State for the Environment* [1978] J.P.L. 554—dwelling-houses—conditions requiring provision of playground and shopping centre).

Even though such a condition is relevant to the proposed development, it might additionally benefit other activities which have no connection with the development. Thus a condition requiring the expansion of an existing car park in connection with a public house extension could well benefit persons other than users of the public house. The test to apply in such cases is whether the condition can be justified by the needs of the development itself. If so, then the existence of other incidental benefits can be ignored (*Westminster Corporation* v. *L.N.W.R.* [1905] A.C. 426). If however the condition specifies something to be done over and above what the development requires then it is wholly void: (*Webb* v. *Minister of Housing* [1965] 1 W.L.R. 755; see Wade, pp. 364–372).

It has also been said that a condition, and indeed the reasons for any planning decision, must be related to the use of the land. The main authority for this is *Mixnam's Properties Ltd.* v. *Chertsey U.D.C.* [1965] A.C. 735. This case turned upon the Caravan Sites and Control of Development Act 1960. The House of Lords held that conditions attached to a caravan site licence should not be concerned with such matters as security of tenure and rent limits, since these did not relate to the use of the land. However the purposes of this Act are not as wide as those of planning (see *Esdell Caravan Parks Ltd.* v. *Hemel Hempstead R.D.* [1966] 1 Q.B. 895).

In any event the notion of "use" of land is wide and imprecise. Any human activity on land can be described as a use of that land (see above, p. 54). This concept does not in itself substantially limit the powers of planners. There may be cases, for example, matters of finance or title, which can plausibly be regarded as unrelated to the use of the land, but there seems to be no policy reason for excluding such matters from the scope of planning. It is clear that a planning condition can limit the class of persons who can occupy premises (*Fawcett Properties* v. *Bucks C.C.* [1961] A.C. 636—persons connected or formerly connected with local agriculture; *Wakelin* v. *Secretary of State & St. Albans District Council* [1978] J.P.L. 769—occupation of dwelling-houses limited to close relatives or members of household staff of neighbouring buildings). This kind of condition can be said indirectly to affect the use of the land in that it may affect the range of activities which the neighbourhood supports. The purpose of the *Fawcett* condition, for example, was to keep out commuters and thereby preserve the rural character of the neighbourhood (see also *Allnatt London Properties* v. *Middlesex C.C.* (1964) 15 P. & C.R. 288). It has also been held that the cost of the proposed development can be taken into account. Indeed to suggest otherwise would be unrealistic and artificial. (See *Sovmots Investments* v. *Secretary of State* [1976] 2 W.L.R. 73, 82; *Hambleton and Chiddingfold Parish Councils* v. *Secretary of State for the Environment* [1976] J.P.L. 506; *cf. J. Murphy & Sons Ltd.* v. *Secretary of State* [1973] 1 W.L.R. 560; *Niarchos (London) Ltd.* v. *Secretary of State* (1978) 245 E.G. 847; *Walters* v. *Welsh Secretary* (1979) 249 E.G. 244; *Brighton B.C.* v. *Secretary of State* [1979] J.P.L. 173.)

The concept seems to produce arbitrary distinctions. For

example, *R.* v. *Hillingdon B.C., ex p. Royco Homes Ltd.* [1974] Q.B. 720 left open the question whether planning permission could be refused to a private developer on the ground that the land should be used for public housing. Upon a use of land analysis the answer is probably that this would be *ultra vires* although even here the imaginative planner might be able to suggest land use implications. There is no doubt that housing need is itself a legitimate consideration (see *Clyde & Co. Ltd.* v. *Secretary of State* (above)). Thus planning permission can be refused to a developer whose plans do not physically provide the sort of housing which the council wants. Moreover it is apparent from *Royco* that conditions can be attached prescribing design standards analogous to those used for public housing.

Is there therefore any good reason why the same policy cannot be achieved by either reserving land for public housing or granting permission on condition that the land be developed by a semi-public housing assosication? (see [1974] J.P.L. 507 particularly at p. 513 and *David Lowe* v. *Musselburgh* (1974) S.L.T. 5).

The land use test does however have the merit of excluding contingent matters of individual behaviour from the attentions of planners. Thus a gypsy site and a student commune cannot be prohibited merely because the occupiers are behaving badly (see *Birmingham Corporation* v. *Minister of Housing and Habib Ullah* [1964] 1 Q.B. 178, 188). There is no causal relationship between the behaviour of the occupiers and the nature of the activity. By contrast a discothèque by definition involves noise and thus can be refused planning permission or a condition limiting the level or duration of the noise can be imposed.[6]

Finally, a land use implication can often be discovered in connection with matters which do not in themselves affect land use. Thus as authority can take into account commercial competition and refuse planning permission to construct a "hypermarket" upon the grounds that the new development might adversely affect other shops and cause a decline in both the appearance and the level of facilities of a nearby town or village (see *J. Sainsbury & Co. Ltd.* v. *Secretary of State for the Environment* [1978] J.P.L. 379).

It must be remembered that once a consideration is recognised as relevant a court cannot interfere with the weight which the authority gives to it. As long as there is some evidence to support a decision it cannot be set aside in circumstances short of gross unreasonableness (see *Coleen Properties* v. *Minister of Housing* [1971] 1 W.L.R. 433).

Failure to Take Relevant Factors into Account

Problems of this kind commonly arise where an authority adopts a general policy and applies it uniformly to all individual cases. Whatever merits the policy itself may have, this is unlawful. A discretion must be exercised in the light of the facts of each application. Thus an authority must not automatically reject all applications which conflict with the development plan, nor do the same pending formulation of a development plan. Similarly an authority cannot treat itself as bound either by an appeal decision of the Secretary of State or by a policy circular. Only statute or a court decision can impose absolute obligations.

The limits of this doctrine must be emphasised. There is no reason why an authority cannot adopt a policy and apply it in all but the most exceptional cases. There is as a matter of law no automatic presumption that the development plan must be obeyed (*Enfield L.B.C.* v. *Secretary of State for the Environment* (1974) 233 E.G. 53) but an authority can adopt such a presumption if it so wishes. All it has to show is that it has considered other relevant matters (*Stringer* v. *Minister of*

Housing [1970] 1 W.L.R. 1281). "Although [an Authority] is not obliged to consider every application before it with an open mind it must at least keep its mind ajar" (see de Smith, p. 275).

However a consistent rejection of a given kind of application may justify a court inferring that there has been an unlawful fettering of discretion (*Macbeth* v. *Ashley* (1874) L.R. 2 H.L. (S.C.) 352, 357).

Unreasonableness

In many cases the terms unreasonableness and irrelevance overlap in the sense that decision is unreasonable because it is based upon some irrelevant consideration. However the two notions are distinct (*e.g. Hall & Co.* v. *Shoreham U.D.C.*, (below).

To allow judicial review for unreasonableness comes close to inviting the courts to intervene with the merits and policy of a decision. In order to avoid this danger the courts have consistently emphasised that unreasonableness has a special meaning unrelated to the hypothetical standards of the man on the Clapham omnibus (see Lord Denning's judgment in *Secretary of State for Education and Science* v. *Tameside M.B.C.* [1976] 3 W.L.R. 641 at 652–653). A decision is unreasonable only if it is arbitrary or capricious or "so unreasonable that no reasonable authority could ever have come to it."

This formula derives from the judgment of Lord Greene M.R. in *Associated Provincial Picture Houses* v. *Wednesbury Corporation* [1948] 1 K.B. 223, 229–231. It is doubtful however whether it does any more than emphasise that unreasonable means "very unreasonable," and it may be that the United States doctrine, that a decision will not be set aside if its merits are "fairly debateable" provides a better test.[7]

Indeed the courts have set aside decisions as unreasonable which could only by a gross distortion of language be described as capricious, such as a statutory instrument which purported to exclude the jurisdiction of the courts (*Customs & Excise Commissioners* v. *Cure & Deeley* [1962] 1 Q.B. 340). Do the local authority decisions in *Hall* (below) and *Royco* (above) really deserve to be stigmatised as "unreasonable" in Lord Greene's sense? The courts will regard as "unreasonable" a decision which they think either unduly harsh (*cf. R.* v. *Barnsley Metropolitan Borough Council ex p. Hook* [1976] 1 W.L.R. 1052), or which without express or necessarily implied statutory authority violates judicial presumptions against interference with traditional freedoms of person or property.

Hall & Co. v. *Shoreham U.D.C.* [1964] 1 W.L.R. 240 is the high water mark of this approach. Permission was granted to erect industrial plant on condition that the applicant constructed at his own expense a public road across his frontage. It was held that the condition was void, not because it was imposed for irrelevant reasons (there were adequate planning reasons because of the traffic generated by his development) but because it was unreasonable. Under highways legislation the same purpose could be achieved but subject to the payment of compensation. The Court of Appeal applied the presumption that property rights should not be taken away without compensation and drew the conclusion that Parliament intended the authority to proceed under the highways legislation.

More recently the application of this presumption has been severely restricted. The presumption against deprivation of property rights begs the question, what is meant by a "right"? This was recognised in *Hall* by Wilmer L.J. who emphasised that since there is no general right to develop land it cannot be argued that the presumption applies in all cases where the use of land is severely restricted.

This was taken further by the House of Lords in *Westminster Bank* v. *Minister of Housing* [1970] 2 W.L.R. 645 (above,

p. 6). Lord Reid emphasised that there is no general right to compensation for the refusal of planning permission and that therefore the applicant had not been deprived of anything. It was moreover reasonable for an authority to choose the cheapest method of proceeding and thereby to avoid paying compensation (see also *Mixnam's Properties Ltd.* v. *Chertsey U.D.C.* [1965] A.C. 735, 754–755).

Similar reasoning has been applied in a rather different context. There is a line of Divisional Court cases where it has been held that a planning condition can deprive the developer of "existing rights" over his land. (*City of London Corporation* v. *Secretary of State* (1973) 23 P. & C.R. 169; *Kingston-on-Thames B.C.* v. *Secretary of State* [1973] 1 W.L.R. 1549; *A.I. & P. (Stratford) Ltd.* v. *Tower Hamlets B.C.* [1976] J.P.L. 234; *Penwith D.C.* v. *Secretary of State* [1977] J.P.L. 371. See also *Prossor* v. *Minister of Housing* (1968) 67 L.G.R. 109). Existing rights are those conferred by the planning legislation itself and include activities which are not development, activities exempt from the need for permission, activities covered by an earlier permission and activities time-barred from enforcement, albeit this last category may be distinguishable as being "unlawful," the bar against enforcement being merely procedural (see *L.T.S.S. Print & Supply Ltd.* v. *Hackney B.C.* (above, p. 75). See further (1972) 36 Conv. 421).

The Act provides machinery for prohibiting the exercise of existing rights which requires the payment of compensation (sections 45, 51). Thus existing rights cases can be excluded from the *Westminster Bank* principle in as much as they fall outside the general proposition that compensation is not payable for planning restrictions. The Act itself gives these rights a special status by imposing special revocation procedures and a compensation requirement. It is sometimes stated that these rights are not really taken away because the applicant can always choose not to implement the planning permission with the onerous condition, and therefore if he does implement it he has voluntarily abandoned his existing right (see [1973] J.P.L. 685). This is entirely unsatisfactory except in the case where the terms of the developer's own application for planning permission are inconsistent with his existing rights. The question is whether a landowner should be forced to make such a choice.

It is submitted that these cases, all of them at first instance, should not be followed and that existing rights cannot be restricted by a planning condition. There is authority in favour of this (*Allnatt London Properties* v. *Middlesex C.C.* (1964) 15 P. & C.R. 288; *Hartnell* v. *Minister of Housing* [1965] A.C. 1134; *Esdell Caravan Parks* v. *Hemel Hempstead R.D.C.* [1966] 1 Q.B. 895, 923–924; *East Barnet U.D.C.* v. *B.T.C.* [1962] 2 Q.B. 484). Of these *Hartnell*, the most weighty, has been explained as involving specific restrictions placed upon planning powers by the Caravan Sites and Control Development Act 1960. There are indications in Lord Reid's speech to this effect (at p. 1157) but the reasoning of the others was of more general application (see pp. 1166–1167 and 1172–1173).

What authority if any has *Hall's* case retained? It can be distinguished from *Westminster Bank* as involving not merely the refusal of permission but the expropriation of the applicant's entire beneficial interest by requiring him to dedicate land for public purposes (*cf. Hoveringham Gravels Ltd.* v. *Secretary of State* [1975] 2 W.L.R. 897 at 905). In this exceptional class of case the presumption in favour of compensation may still be important. The matter thus depends upon reasonableness in the particular circumstances rather than upon *a priori* assumptions about vested rights. *R.* v. *Hillingdon B.C., ex p. Royco Homes Ltd.* [1974] Q.B. 720 is consistent with this. There a developer was granted permission for the construction of dwelling-houses, subject to a condition that he allocated them to persons on the waiting list for council houses. This was held to be unreasonable, as an excessively onerous interference with property rights since the developer was effectively being required to shoulder the burden of a public housing authority (compare *Hitchins (Robert) Builders* v. *Secretary of State* [1978] J.P.L. 554).

There have been no other cases of successful challenge to planning decisions for unreasonableness *per se*. It is probable however that an unenforceable condition is invalid as is one that could be broken due to factors beyond the developer's control *Kent C.C.* v. *Kingsway Investments* [1971] A.C. 72).

In one situation the Secretary of State's view is arguably too cautious. Influenced no doubt by another traditional presumption, that the payment of money be authorised by clear statutory language (*R.* v. *Bowman* [1898] 1 Q.B. 633; *R.* v. *Birmingham Licensing Planning Committee, ex p. Kennedy* [1972] 2 Q.B. 140) he has consistently held that payment cannot be demanded in exchange for a planning permission (see [1977] J.P.L. 691–692). While it is true that a developer cannot be required to pay for planning permission, there seems to be no reason why a condition should not require him either to provide infrastructure in connection with the proposed development or to make a payment in lieu. The same is true of the provision of incidental facilities such as car parks. Conditions can certainly impose expensive positive obligations upon a developer such as to provide a car park, for use in connection with his development (*e.g. Kingston-upon-Thames B.C.* v. *Secretary of State* [1973] 1 W.L.R. 1549) and there may be a policy justification for the authority preferring for example to expand an existing public car park rather than to create a new one. In such a case it is difficult to see why a developer should not be required to make a contribution, the validity of the requirement being determined by the relationship between what he is required to pay and the needs of his development.

This approach has been taken in the United States in connection with subdivision approval for residential development (see *Re Lake Secor Development Co.* 252 N.Y.S. 809 (Sup. Ct. 1931) also (1972) 14 *William and Mary Law Review* 249). The various state jurisdictions differ as to the required connection between the payment and the development, but one criterion which could be adopted is that the cost must be "specifically and uniquely attributable to the proposed development" (see *Rosen* v. *Village of Downers Grove* 167 N.E. 2d 230. (I.U. 1960).

Remedies

The principles governing review of discretion reveal that the courts are unwilling to interfere with the decisions of planning authorities upon grounds other than procedure. Few challenges have been successful and where an application has succeeded upon its merits the court's refusal to sever a condition has sometimes turned the victory into a Pyrrhic one.

The other method of challenging a local authority planning decision is by way of appeal to the Secretary of State who can, as we have seen, take a broader view than the courts.

The appeals procedure will be discussed in Chapter 8. We can however discuss now the question of choice of method of challenge.

Where the complainant is a person other than the applicant he has no choice. His only legal remedy lies through the courts. Thus an unconditional grant of planning permission can be challenged only by way of judicial review.

The applicant must however choose the correct remedy. He may apply for certiorari to quash a decision, a declaration to declare its invalidity, prohibition or an injunction to present enforcement of an unlawful decision, or mandamus to require the authority to make a decision in accordance with the law.

E

Mandamus can also expose the fact that an existing decision is a nullity (see *R.* v. *Paddington Valuation Officer, ex p. Peachey Properties Ltd.* [1966] 1 Q.B. 380).

These remedies thus overlap in terms of the result they achieve. The task of choosing the right remedy involves a detailed balancing of the properties of each one in relation to the facts of the case. The remedies have developed historically along separate lines and none are specifically designed for the task of controlling discretionary decisions. Thus *locus standi* requirements differ, that for certiorari being the most generous (see above, p. 32). None of the remedies can require the authority to decide in any particular way. At best the court can declare a decision void and issue mandamus to require the authority to reconsider the matter.

Until recently the declaration was the procedure most often used in planning cases. However now that it is established that certiorari also lies there is nothing to be gained by using the declaration. The recent reforms in the procedure for seeking certiorari (R.S.C., Ord. 53 (S.I. 1977 No. 1955)) have abolished the procedural limitations—no interlocutory process or cross-examination—which made certiorari unsatisfactory as a remedy against abuse of discretion (see Law Com. No. 73 (1976)).[8] We have already seen that the *locus standi* requirement for a declaration is narrow. Moreover interim relief is available in certiorari cases but still, apparently, not in the case of the declaration. Finally the declaration is not available where a decision is voidable as opposed to void (*Punton* v. *Minister of Pensions (No. 2)* [1964] 1 W.L.R. 226) since the declaration cannot quash but merely states the existing legal position. Thus certiorari avoids the difficulty of distinguishing void from voidable decisions (see n. [4] above).

The consequences of choosing the wrong remedy are alleviated by the new procedure for judicial review. An applicant can now under Order 53 seek any of the remedies either cumulatively or in the alternative and can apply to alter the remedy during the course of proceedings (see rr. 1 and 3 (4)).

However the new procedure does not exclude those available under the existing law. It merely provides an alternative procedure. Thus an applicant can still apply to the Chancery Division for a declaration.[9] In most cases however the new procedure will be more favourable. It does however have one drawback from the applicant's point of view in that leave to apply for the remedy is necessary (r. 3). *Locus standi* has to be determined at this stage and the rules do not make it clear what standing is required, merely stipulating that the applicant have "a sufficient interest" in the matter (see note (1978) 41 M.L.R. 437, 440).

In the case of certiorari, the new procedure is in one respect more restrictive than the old. The previous time limit of six months is replaced by one of three months. However the court may refuse to grant the remedy outside this limit (and in cases of other remedies where there has been undue delay), only upon grounds of hardship and "good administration" (r. 4). It seems therefore that the court's general discretion to refuse relief where for example the delay is the applicant's own fault is curtailed.

Where the applicant himself wishes to challenge either a refusal of or a conditional grant of permission he is faced with the further dilemma whether to apply immediately to the court or to appeal to the Secretary of State under section 36. Judicial review is not excluded merely by the existence of a statutory right of appeal, but the court can in its discretion refuse to hear a case where it considers that recourse to the Secretary of State would be more appropriate, for example where the issue is not purely one of law.

If the applicant appeals to the Secretary of State he can still challenge legal aspects of both the Secretary's and the local authority's decision by applying to the court for review of the Secretary of State's decision. This does not involve the general judicial review remedies, but is governed by special statutory machinery (see below, pp. 179–183).

It must however be borne in mind that the Secretary of State's powers are wider than those of the court. The court's powers are limited to quashing the decision and remitting it to the authority. The Secretary of State on the other hand can strike out or remodel the condition or grant a fresh planning permission. He has in effect the same powers as the local planning authority and can thus reconsider the matter *ab initio* (section 36 (3)). By the same token the Secretary of State could impose more onerous restrictions upon the permission, or grant a more limited form of permission (see *Kent C.C.* v. *Secretary of State* (1976) 33 P. & C.R. 70).

Despite the fact that the Secretary of State combines the judicial role of appellate tribunal with his administrative task of policy-making and implementation there is no evidence that he is less solicitous towards individual property rights than is the Divisional Court. Indeed many of the cases are examples of his underestimating his powers.

More generally we have seen in this chapter (and will see further in Chapter 7) that there is little evidence in the cases since *Hall* v. *Shoreham* of the alleged judicial bias in favour of private property rights and against legislative interference. (*cf.* (1974) 37 M.L.R. 134 and Griffiths, *The Politics of the Judiciary* (1977)). Quite the reverse—in cases where a genuine choice of principle was available (*e.g.* the *Westminster Bank, Kingsway* and *Kingston-on-Thames* cases) the courts have consistently chosen a solution in favour of the planners. It may be that the *ultra vires* doctrine is an unsatisfactory conceptual foundation upon which to develop a system of external controls over planning decisions since as Professor de Smith has pointed out judicial review is "inevitably sporadic and peripheral" (p. 3). The inherent uncertainty of the law has also provided opportunity for fluctuations of judicial attitude both between individual judges (*vide* the many dissenting judgments in administrative law cases) and over periods of time (see [1978] J.P.L. 512).

It may be that a special administrative court with broader terms of reference than are presently available would provide a more appropriate forum for settling disputes between citizen and planning authority. This already exists in the form of the Lands Tribunal in respect of some land use matters. At least a strengthened and extended tribunal of this kind would release the Divisional Court of some of its heavy and heterogeneous work load.

Notes

1 Section 59 imposes a general obligation to take trees into account. See also Countryside Act 1968, section 11.

2 In some cases the highways authority may give binding directions. GDO 1977, art. 12.

3 Compare Garner, *Administrative Law* (4th ed.), pp. 113–154; Wade, Part IV; de Smith, Chap. 6. See also [1976] C.L.J. 272.

4 There is one other ground of review—error of law on the face of the record. This has limited application in the planning context being more appropriate to the decisions of tribunals deciding detailed questions of law rather than to the exercise of discretion. Error of law makes a decision only voidable as opposed to void and certiorari is probably the only remedy. The distinction between *ultra vires* and error of law is however important in connection with the statutory machinery for challenging the Secretary of State's decision (see below, p. 181). It is arguable that *Anisminic* v. *Foreign Compensation Commission* [1969] 2 A.C. 147 has in any event eradicated the distinction in that it was decided there that "irrelevant considerations" make a decision *ultra vires* and void. All errors of law could be categorised under that head. See Wade, pp. 257–264; Diplock (1974) 33 C.L.J. 233; Gould [1970] P.L. 358. But see *R.* v. *Southampton JJ.* [1976] Q.B. 11. It is sometimes maintained that other defects make a decision

only voidable (*cf. R.* v. *Secretary of State, ex p. Osler* [1977] Q.B. 122) including abuse of discretion. Since the conceptual and constitutional basis of judicial review is the ultra vires doctrine this is unsupportable. However whether the logical consequences of nullity are consistently applied is a different question. See Wade, pp. 296–304; 83 L.Q.R. 499, 84 L.Q.R. 95, 93 L.Q.R. 8. *Quaere* how to classify a decision vitiated by lack of evidence. See *Coleen* v. *Minister of Housing* [1971] 1 W.L.R. 433. It is suggested that this is best regarded as an example of unreasonableness.

5 See Wade, pp. 222–226. See also *Durayappah* v. *Fernando* [1967] 2 A.C. 337.

5a *cf. Wimpey (George) Ltd.* v. *New Forest District Council* (1979) 250 E.G. 249.

6 Readers might consider the following: (i) can the desirability of creating or maintaining employment be taken into account? (*cf. Clyde & Co.* case (above)) (ii) Could permission for a betting shop be refused on moral grounds or because of the risk of attracting criminals? (iii) Can an authority limit the occupation of dwelling-houses to local industrial workers or forbid occupation by students? (iv) Can a condition be attached to a restaurant regulating the provision of liquor, or forbidding topless waitresses?

7 See [1975] 24 *Catholic University Law Review* 294.

8 But see *George* v. *Secretary of State* (1979) 250 E.G. 339.

9 But *cf. Uppal* v. *Home Office, The Times,* Nov. 11, 1978.

Chapter 5

THE LEGAL EFFECT OF PLANNING PERMISSION

A decision upon an application for planning permission must be notified in writing to the applicant within eight weeks of the date of application (GDO 1977, Art. 7). Failure to comply with the time limit is treated as a refusal of permission from which the applicant may appeal to the Secretary of State (Section 37). The time limit may be extended by agreement but in any event it does not seem to be mandatory so that once an applicant has acted upon an untimely decision he becomes bound by it (*James* v. *Secretary of State for Wales* [1968] A.C. 409).[1]

A planning permission runs with the land and will bind and benefit all persons from time to time interested in the land (section 33 (1)). Applications and permissions must be registered in a public register kept by the local planning authority (section 34) and it is to this conveyancers have recourse when investigating the planning implications of a transaction. There is no convenient way of discovering what planning rights apply to other land in the neighbourhood of that being purchased. The validity of a permission is not affected by failure to register or by an incorrect registration.[2]

There are, however, several ways in which the planning permission can be brought to an end.

First, it will lapse if the development is not commenced within a statutory time limit of five years (section 41). This

113

provision introduced in 1968 was designed to combat land hoarding and includes special rules dealing with outline permissions and with those granted before 1969. A development is "commenced" for this purpose when any of certain prescribed activities take place (section 43 (2)). These include such matters as digging foundations, or laying roads (but not merely demolishing existing buildings) and as long as they are broadly related to the proposed development need not conform exactly with the plans which formed the subject of application (*cf. Spackman* v. *Secretary of State for the Environment* [1977] 1 All E.R. 257).

The converse case of a development started but not finished within the time limit is dealt with by section 44. Here the authority may serve a "completion notice" which states that the planning permission will cease to have effect within a specified time which must be at least 12 months. The notice must be confirmed by the Secretary of State. The effect of the notice is that the permission remains valid in respect of development carried out before the time limit but any development thereafter will require a fresh application for permission. The original permission can however be renewed if application is made before the time limit expires, and a simplified procedure is available for such applications.

The authority may also revoke a planning permission before it is implemented (section 45) and after implementation can prohibit any use or require the alteration or renewal of any building or works (section 51). Both these drastic powers require the payment of compensation and are exercised only sparingly.

Apart from these specific powers a temporary planning permission can be granted by means of a suitable condition and the Act empowers the authority to require that the land be restored to its original state at the end of the prescribed time (section 30 (1) (*b*)). Moreover an authority can grant permission personal to the applicant if for example an exception to a general policy is called for on humanitarian grounds. Thus a non-conforming business use could be permitted on condition that it remain personal to the applicant as being his sole means of livelihood.

A planning permission can also be extinguished by conduct. Where a permission has been implemented the situation is the same as that discussed in Chapter 2 in connection with the abandonment of a use. Thus the benefit of a permission is lost where there is a subsequent change of use, or the erection of a building, or evidence of abandonment.

The position is more complicated where the permission has not been implemented. As a general principle a person can hold as many alternative planning permissions as the authority are prepared to grant him. However once he has implemented one of them the benefit of the others is lost to the extent that they are inconsistent with the one implemented. The question whether they are inconsistent is one of construction and as we will see intention is not relevant. A planning permission is lost if the developer does any act which is inconsistent with it. Thus in *Slough Estates Ltd*. v. *Slouth B.C.* [1969] 2 Ch. 305 (upheld in the House of Lords on a different basis [1971] A.C. 958) the developer was uncertain of the scope of his planning permission and accepted compensation in respect of the refusal of a later application. It subsequently wished to rely upon the planning permission and was prepared to repay the compensation since the land with benefit of the original permission would be worth considerably more. It was held that the acceptance of compensation had extinguished the original permission.[3]

It is thus important to determine what acts can be treated as inconsistent with a planning permission. Prima facie an applicant can combine the benefits of any planning permission he holds. Thus in *Lucas* v. *Dorking R.D.C.* (1964) 62 L.G.R. 491 the applicant held two permissions in respect of the same site, one for 28 high-density houses, the other for six larger dwellings. It was held that a planning permission does not in itself *require* a development to be carried out but merely prevents it from being illegal. Thus there was nothing to prevent the developer from building some of each kind of house as long as in either case the stipulated number was not exceeded. The resulting development of course bore little relation to what the authority had in mind.

It has been argued that *Copeland B.C.* v. *Secretary of State for the Environment* (above, p. 51) weakens the authority of *Lucas* in that it requires a permission to be implemented as a whole (see Purdue, p. 185). *Copeland* however held only that the construction of a house constitutes a single indivisible "building operation" so that if the roof were made of the wrong materials the whole house would have been built without permission. The question is one of law and not of construction of the planning permission. Thus it does not follow that everything within a given planning permission is a single act of development. It would for example be absurd to treat a permission for the construction of 200 dwellings as a permission for one building operation. Indeed the position of a resident on an uncompleted housing estate would be extremely precarious if the *Copeland* reasoning was thus extended. The questions of what is a "building operation" and what operations are authorised by a given permission are entirely separate ones.

The *Lucas* principle can easily be avoided by drafting a planning permission to make it clear that it is exercisable only as an alternative to any other planning rights which may exist in respect of the site. Thus in *Pilkington* v. *Secretary of State for the Environment* [1973] 1 W.L.R. 1527 the developer held three separate permissions each for a single bungalow on different parts of the same site. It was held that he could build only one bungalow rather than three, since in each case the permission provided that the bungalow was to be the only one on the site (see also *Ellis* v. *Worcestershire C.C.* (1961) 12 P. & C.R. 178; *Langley* v. *Warwick D.C.* (1974) 29 P. & C.R. 358).

An unresolved question is whether a planning permission is lost for good when the developer acts inconsistently with it, or whether it is merely suspended. If it is permanently lost then a subsequent purchaser may be prejudiced because the planning rights as disclosed by the register have been destroyed by events of which he is unaware and has no means of finding out. The register itself confers no protection on anyone. As against this it is desirable from the planning authority's point of view to treat the earlier permission as lost, in that changed circumstances may make its implementation undesirable. Moreover it is clear that a permission which has been implemented is permanently lost by abandonment or extinction and there is no reason why the position should be different in the case of unimplemented permissions. Where the permission is for a change of use it is certainly lost for good, the permission being in respect of the act of change and not the use itself.

Construction of Planning Permissions

It is settled that extrinsic aids cannot generally be used to construe a planning permission. Nor is the intention of the parties relevant (*ex p. Reinisch* (1971) 22 P. & C.R. 1022). A planning permission is a public document which affects all persons concerned with the land. It would therefore be highly inconvenient for conveyancing purposes if surrounding circumstances existing at the time of the grant were relevant in determining its meaning. Moreover the *contra proferentem* principle applicable to the construction of private documents does not apply to planning permissions (*Crisp from the Fens Ltd.* v. *Rutland C.C.* (1950) 1 P. & C.R. 48).

It is thus essential to determine what documents constitute a planning permission. The council grants permission by means of a resolution taken at a council or committee meeting. The GDO provides that permission must be notified in writing to the applicant but there is no requirement that the permission itself be in writing. However, it was held in *R.* v. *Yeovil B.C. ex p. Trustees of Elim Pentacostal Church Yeovil* (1971) 23 P. & C.R. 39 that the notification document constitutes the actual planning permission. If this is so then the terms of the council's resolution cannot be considered at all (see also *Slough Estates* v. *Slough B.C. (No. 2)* [1969] 2 Ch. 305). This somewhat artificial rule is out of step with general principle as regards local government decision-making and has been subject to consider-able criticism (see Albery (1974) 90 L.Q.R. 351; Garner [1972] J.P.L. 194). The point was not necessary to the decision in Yeovil. The council had resolved to authorise its town clerk to grant permission for a youth centre subject to evidence of an agreement concerning car parking. Before the decision was notified the council changed its mind and resolved to refuse permission. It was held that no planning permission existed until the decision had been notified and thus the council's *volte face* was effective. The decision to the same effect in the *Slough* case was followed but without referring to the fact that the earlier decision turned on the pre-1948 law which, unlike the present GDO, did not distinguish between the permission and its notification (see *Albery, loc. cit.,* p. 353). Moreover because of the terms of the resolution it was held that the council had not granted any planning permission but had delegated the power to do so to the town clerk.

From the constitutional point of view it is worth preserving the principle that a local government body acts through its resolutions since these take place at meetings of which the minutes are available to the public[4] (L.G.A. 1972, section 228 (1)). It is both artificial and undesirable to prevent the minutes from being looked at as part of the permission although light of later cases this one is no longer good law. The authority professional conveyancers very well. It is at least clear from *Norfolk C.C.* v. *Secretary of State* [1973] 1 W.L.R. 1400 that a notification is ineffective unless a resolution to grant permission has in fact been made. There the council had resolved to refuse permission but the notification stated that it had been granted. t was held that no permission existed (see above, p. 37). The esolution must therefore be examined at least to this extent. 3hould the position be any different where for example the notification omits a condition?

It is clear that other documents can be looked at only if the permission expressly refers to them thus incorporating them by reference (*Miller-Mead* v. *Minister of Housing* [1963] 2 Q.B. 196; *Wilson* v. *West Sussex C.C.* [1963] 2 Q.B. 764; *Slough Estates* cases (above)). Thus a notification will often state that permission is granted "on the terms of the application and any relevant correspondence."

Even this concession raises conveyancing problems and it may be available only in the case of disputes between the original parties.

There is some authority that surrounding circumstances can be looked at if the documents are ambiguous or erroneous. In *Kent* v. *Guildford R.D.C.* (1959) 11 P. & C.R. 255 the appellants were granted permission for up to 35 caravans on a site. They later received a second permission for up to 60 caravans on a defined part of the site. They subsequently attempted to combine the two permissions and parked up to 99 vans over the whole site. It was held that the history and background of the application could be looked at including the state of the land. From this it was clear that the second permission was to be treated as superseding the first so that the limit of 60 vans must be construed as governing the whole site. However what the court was really doing here was to have regard to the intention of the authority and it may be that in the in the traditions of English property law it serves the interests of could in any event have achieved their aim by a more clearly drafted permission and it is surely desirable that they should be compelled to do so (see also *R.* v. *Secretary of State for the Environment and Another, ex p. Reinisch* (1978) 22 P. & C.R. 1022).

Moreover the court will lean in favour of validity and when faced with ambiguity or uncertainty will construe a permission in the light of the authority's legitimate policy. It will be rejected for uncertainty only if the court can discover no sensible meaning at all. This is particularly important in the case of conditions. Thus in *Fawcett Properties Ltd.* v. *Bucks C.C.* [1961] A.C. 636 a condition was upheld which provided that the "occupation" of two cottages "shall be limited to persons whose employment or latest employment is or was employment in agriculture or in any industry mainly dependent upon agriculture." The House of Lords limited the scope of this extremely vague formula by construing it as referring only to local agriculture and thus conforming to the council's Green Belt policy.

A final problem of construction concerns the possibility of a planning permission containing implied conditions or limitations. The Act does not authorise a local planning authority to impose "limitations" at all although it does so in the case of development orders made by the Secretary of State (section 24). The enforcement provisions do however make it clear that non-compliance with a limitation is a breach of planning control (section 87 (2) (3); See also section 243 (5)).

It has been held however that express limitations attached to a grant of planning permission can be valid. In *Wilson* v. *West Sussex C.C.* [1963] 2 Q.B. 764 permission was granted for the erection of "an agriculture cottage." The authority later imposed an express *condition* confining occupation to persons engaged in agriculture. The issue was whether this derogated from the original grant thus entitling the developer to compensation (*cf.* section 45). It was held that the original permission expressly limited occupation of the cottage to agricultural persons and thus the developer incurred no loss by virtue of the condition. The Court of Appeal doubted however whether conditions or limitations could be implied into a planning permission bearing in mind the power to impose express conditions.[5]

It appears however that the doctrine of implied limitations is alive and well. In *Kwik Save Discount Group Ltd.* v. *Secretary of State for Wales and Another* (1979) 37 P. & C.R. 170 permission was granted for the conversion of a workshop on a garage site to a retail salesroom. No condition or express limitation was attached as to what could be sold there. It was held that the building could not be used as a retail supermarket for the sale of groceries. One line of reasoning concerned the planning unit (see above, p. 66). Independently of this however it was implied that the building although separately occupied could be used only for the sale of products connected with the garage. This decision seems on principle to be objectionable in as much as it condones imprecisely-drafted planning permissions.

The distinction between a condition or limitation is that a limitation defines the nature of the permitted use while a condition imposes additional obligations. The difference between them is, like that between conditions and limitations in property law, sometimes merely semantic.[6] Thus in *Wilson* the same result was achieved by both the original limitation and the later condition (see *Petticoat Lane Rentals* v. *Secretary of State for the Environment* [1971] 1 W.L.R. 1112). It is tempting to extend the analogy with determinable and conditional interests by suggesting that breach of a limitation but not of a condition automatically brings the planning permission to an end. This would serve a useful policy function by allowing the authority to choose how stringent a form of control to impose.

Other Controls

It must be remembered that many uses of land are subject to special controls in addition to those imposed by the development control machinery. They are outside the scope of this book, but some of them can be briefly mentioned. The 1971 Act imposes special controls over industrial and office development, buildings of historic or architectural interest, trees, advertisements and waste land. There are also controls over caravan sites (Caravan Sites and Control of Development Act 1960), forestry (Forestry Act 1967), ancient monuments (Historic Buildings and Ancient Monuments Act 1953; see circular 53/77), and oil refineries (Petroleum and Submarine Pipelines Act 1975). Finally, approval under public health legislation is required for some kinds of building operation. Application for this "building by-law" consent is normally made at the same time and to the same authority as the application for planning permission.

The relationship between planning permission and the Community Land Act 1975 can conveniently be mentioned here. It will be recalled that the 1975 Act empowers local authorities to acquire land suitable for development. The intention however is not to supersede the development control system. First there are many classes of development which are exempt from the compulsory acquisition power (see Community Land (Excepted Development) Regulations 1976 (No. 331)). Secondly, even when the Act is fully implemented the local authority may not in fact acquire all development land. The Act imposes a duty on local authorities to "take steps to acquire." The Secretary of State has a discretion whether to confirm a compulsory purchase order and the way in which he exercises this is the ultimate determinant of the scope of the Act.

Moreover the flow of applications for planning permission

will be one of the main ways by which a local authority will be able to find out what land in its area is suitable for development (see section 17 (2)). (Development which is within the powers of compulsory acquisition is called "relevant development.") [7]

It is however necessary to prevent private development taking place until the local authority makes up its mind what to do under its Community Land Act powers. To this end machinery is provided for "suspending planning permissions for relevant development" so that they cannot be implemented until the authority has been given a reasonable time to consider the case. The rules depend upon the time when application was made or permission granted and are set out in the standard textbooks. A brief summary will be attempted here (see 1975 Act, ss. 19–22 and Sched. 7).

There are four cases to be considered. First, permissions granted before September 12, 1974 (the day of the White Paper announcing the Community Land Bill) are not affected. These are "excepted" development under the 1976 Regulations. A decision on appeal given after that date is retrospective to the date when permission should have been given.

Secondly, where application for permission was made before the "first appointed day" (which is April 6, 1976) the landowner can serve a "notice of election" upon the authority which requires it to inform him within three months whether it proposes to acquire the land (section 19). Upon service of the notice the permission is suspended until the authority acquires the land. If the authority decides not to acquire or remains silent the permission revives and the authority is deemed to have abandoned its compulsory purchase powers for five years. The authority can however subject its intention not to acquire to conditions. If the authority decides to acquire but subsequently fails to take steps to do so, then after a further period of 12 months it is also deemed to have abandoned its power (for five years) and the permission will revive. The permission will also

F

revive if the compulsory purchase order is not confirmed by the Secretary of State or is quashed by the court.

It must be emphasised that this procedure is permissive in that the land-owner does not have to serve a notice of election. If he chooses not to do so his planning permission is not suspended, but he takes the risk that the authority will at a later date acquire his land.

Thirdly, where the application is made on or after April 6, 1976 the landowner serves no notice but the local authority must inform him whether they intend to acquire the land. If they say that they intend to acquire the permission is suspended. Otherwise they abandon their compulsory acquisition powers for five years. The rules for the revival of permission are thereafter similar to those applicable to the previous case. The authority must inform the landowner of its intentions within the time allowed to the local planning authority for giving notice of its decision on the planning application (eight weeks). It must be remembered that the authority with compulsory purchase powers under the 1975 Act can be any planning authority, *e.g.* both counties and districts within whose territory the land is situated, and also new town development corporations. In Wales there is a special land authority (section 8). Thus the authority which grants planning permission is not necessarily the same as the one which has to decide whether to acquire the land.

The fourth case is as yet hypothetical. The Secretary of State can make an order imposing a duty upon a particular authority to take steps to acquire land in its area. At present authorities have power but no duty so to acquire. The date upon which such an order becomes effective is called the *relevant date*, and will differ from area to area. After the relevant date all planning permissions for relevant development in respect of privately-owned land are automatically suspended regardless of when the application was made, until the land has either been acquired or the acquisition is not confirmed by the Secretary of State (section 21; N.B. subsection (3)).

No relevant dates have yet been specified, and the future of the Community Land Act is problematical. However, judged purely as machinery and ignoring political dogma the Community Land Act 1975 seems to be an admirable piece of legislation.

Having acquired the land the authority is empowered either to carry out development itself or to sell or lease to other persons, subject to the consent of the Secretary of State (section 42). This means that private law methods of controlling development can be called in aid, in particular the law of landlord and tenant which provides sanctions which are both speedier and more effective than those available under the ordinary planning law.[8] The Community Land Act thus recognises the importance of ownership and self-interest as a means to achieving land use goals. Indeed, if this Act does achieve success and acceptance then it may be that the development control system should be dismantled in favour of a more limited method of control based upon the needs of particular localities. A return to zoning may for example be an attractive proposition.

It must be borne in mind when considering the complexities of the planning permission procedure that over 80 per cent. of applications are in fact granted and of the rest another 26 per cent. are granted on appeal. However these figures do not disclose the number of cases where conditions are attached and the power to impose conditions may itself justify the development control machinery. These allow obligations to be imposed which run with the land without the expense and political consequences of compulsory acquisition.

Notes

1 The law governing procedural requirements is extremely uncertain. It seems that there are four possible consequences of a procedural irregularity. First, the resulting decision may be a complete nullity. Secondly, the decision may be voidable in the sense that the court will quash it unless the defect is cured, *e.g.* by estoppel or consent, as in *James*. See also *Wells* v. *Minister of Housing* [1967] 1 W.L.R. 1000. Thirdly, disregard of some procedural requirements has no effect on validity although the obligation can be enforced by mandamus. This was held to apply to a failure to give reasons for imposing a planning condition; see *Brayhead (Ascot) Ltd.* v. *Berks C.C.* [1964] 2 Q.B. 303. Fourthly, it appears that there can be procedural requirements which are neither enforceable nor affect validity (*Brayhead* case above). The distinction between the four classes of procedural defect is based upon the importance of the procedural requirement in the context of the particular statute. The terms "mandatory" and "directory" are not used consistently. "Mandatory" had on occasions been used to describe procedural requirements in each of the first three categories.

2 A condition or limitation attached to a planning permission (other than a deemed permission) is registrable as a local land charge, but only if imposed after the commencement of the Local Land Charges Act 1975 (see ss. 1 (*b*) and (*c*) and 2 (*e*)). The Law Commission had proposed that no such conditions should be registrable (see Law Com. No. 62, paras. 36–39). Before this act it was uncertain whether conditions were registrable. Compare *Rose* v. *Leeds Corporation* [1964] 3 W.L.R. 1393 with *Pyx Granite Co.* v. *Ministry of Housing* [1958] 1 Q.B. 554, 572. In practice they were usually registered. Failure to register a local land charge does not affect its enforceability but entitles a purchaser of the land for valuable consideration to claim compensation (1975 Act, s. 10).

3 Compensation for refusal of planning permission is payable only in special circumstances. See Heap, *An Outline of Planning Law* (7th ed.), pp. 249–279, for a useful account.

4 Council and committee meetings are open to the public subject to a power of exclusion. See L.G.A. 1972, s. 100 (1).

5 Another explanation of *Wilson* is that agricultural use is under the general law a special class of use, so that any change to non-agricultural occupation would automatically be development. It does not follow that a change from any use defined by a permission would be development. Thus if use of a shop was limited to use as a grocer's shop the developer would be in breach of an express limitation if he used the shop as a toyshop, but this would not make the change development (Use Classes Order, above, pp. 68–69).

6 See Megarry and Wade, *The Law of Real Property* (4th. ed.), pp. 74–82.

7 This is not strictly accurate, but is sufficient for the present purpose. In theory an authority can acquire land for all development apart from cases listed in Sched. 1 (see section 15), which exempts development within the GDO and certain development connected with agriculture. The definition of relevant development is somewhat narrower, excluding both Sched. 1 development and development specified by regulations (excepted development). In practice land is unlikely to be acquired for non-relevant development. There is no statutory obligation to consider its acquisition, and it cannot be designated for the purposes of imposing a duty to acquire it.

8 *e.g.* covenants both positive and negative can be imposed and enforced by damages or injunction or re-entry. Where the freehold is assigned, control is more tenuous. Only negative covenants will run with the land (but see Chap. 6 below), and a right of re-entry will be equitable only (Law of Property Act 1925, s. 1 (2)).

Chapter 6

PLANNING BY AGREEMENT

Planning authorities in pursuance of the vision of themselves as
social engineers are making increasing use of agreements with
developers, in order both to achieve positive planning purposes
and to profit from the increase in land values which
development brings about.[1] They believe that such agreements may avoid the limitations placed by the courts upon the
ordinary development control powers.

Examples of such agreements have been conveniently
collated (see Jowell, [1977] J.P.L. 414), and reveal a great
diversity of subject-matter. This includes the provision of
facilities such as shops and playgrounds in connection with
office or residential development, the provision of infrastructure such as drains, and roadworks, the payment of money
towards public services such as car parks, and undertakings to
forfeit existing rights or demolish buildings (see Telling, pp.
183–184). It may be, particularly in view of the courts'
reluctance to interfere with the discretions of planning
authorities, that some of these objectives could be achieved by
means of planning conditions. An agreement does however
have the advantage that its subject-matter need not be related
to the proposed development as such (see *Beaconsfield D.C.* v.
Gams (1974) 234 E.G. 749; see also [1976] J.P.L. 732, 738).
Thus planning authorities are encouraged to use their

bargaining power as a lever to achieve what they call "planning gain." On their side they offer planning permissions or other lucrative benefits or alternatively provide land and services for the developer.

The use of such agreements is justified, narrowly, by claiming that they help to get round problems which would otherwise be a reason for refusing planning permission,[2] and broadly, by invoking the ideal of planners and developers co-operating to achieve social and economic goals. The practice has been hailed as a welcome departure from the "adjudicative dispute resolution" view of planning which sees the planner essentially as an extension of the law of nuisance, towards a goal-orientated "corporatist discretion" model (see Jowell (1977) 30 C.L.P. 63).

Others have pointed to dangers inherent in planning by agreement; for example, the absence of any statutory or common law procedural safeguards such as public consultation (see Grant [1978] J.P.L. 8). At its worst the practice is seen as a form of bribery, and "selling" planning permissions as a modern equivalent of the medieval market in indulgences. It is however generally accepted that the principle of achieving land use goals by agreement is a desirable one (see Report of the Working Party on Local Authority/Private Enterprise Partnership Schemes, HMSO 1972).

However, the law is uncertain, complicated and needs reform. In this chapter we will examine the existing provisions and attempt to identify the problems.

There are three main statutory provisions. First, under the Local Government Act 1972, s. 111, a local authority can "do anything . . . which is calculated to facilitate or is conducive or incidental to the discharge of any of their functions."[3] This section is of limited application in the planning context, because it does not deal with the question of whether an agreement can bind successors in title of the landowner party to it. Apart from special cases which do not concern us here an agreement relating to land is enforceable against successors in title only in equity under the rule in *Tulk* v. *Moxhay* (1848) 18 L.J. Ch. 83).

This applies only to negative obligations and requires that the obligation benefit land owned by the person who wishes to enforce it. The obligation must also be registered as a restrictive covenant under Class D (ii) of the Land Charges Act 1972, failing which it is void against a purchaser of a legal estate.[4] Unless the agreement benefits land owned by the authority it will thus be enforceable only against the original parties (*L.C.C.* v. *Allen* [1914] 3 K.B. 642, 664).

The second provision purports to avoid this difficulty. Section 52 (1) of the 1971 Act authorises local planning authorities "to enter into an agreement with any person interested in land in their area for the purpose of restricting or regulating the development or use of the land." Subsection (2) provides that "an agreement made under this section with any person interested in land may be enforced by the local planning authority against persons deriving title under that person in respect of that land as if the local planning authority were possessed of adjacent land and as if the agreement had been expressed to be made for the benefit of such land."

This section, which traces its history back to section 34 of the Town and Country Planning Act 1932, has received little attention from the courts. Its intention is clearly to enable successors in title to be sued. Its method of doing so is to introduce the fiction that the authority owns benefited land and thus to take advantage of the equitable rules governing restrictive covenants.[5] This indirect method is designed to facilitate conveyancing, since the agreement, being equitable, requires registration (see below, pp. 135–136).

Section 52 (2) raises several technical problems and a strict construction of the provision could severely limit its usefulness. It is unfortunate that Parliament should choose to provide for what are essentially public transactions by incorporating the machinery of private restrictive covenants. Not only is this a notoriously unsatisfactory branch of the law, but the same objectives could have been achieved more directly by making planning agreements binding on successors in title (subject to contrary intention) "as if they were original parties to the agreement" (compare Housing Act 1974, s. 126, below).

First, the formula in subsection (2) does not seem to go far enough in incorporating the *Tulk* v. *Moxhay* doctrine. Equity requires not only the expression of an intention to benefit land owned by the covenantee (which is supplied by section 52 (2)), but also the further requirement that the land be in fact capable of benefiting from the covenant (see Preston and Newsom, *Restrictive Covenants Affecting Freehold Land* (6th. ed.), pp. 70–72, albeit the requirement of benefit is now a liberal one (*Wrotham Park Estates* v. *Parkside Homes Ltd.* [1974] 1 W.L.R. 798).

Where the agreement is one that in principle could benefit defined land (*e.g.* an undertaking not to build) the courts may not balk at inferring that benefit accrues to the authority's imaginary land. However, many obligations, although desirable from a planning point of view, are not in their nature capable of benefiting any defined land at all, for example, to allow public access to the developer's land; but to extend the equitable rules to include these may be asking a judge to make a greater imaginative leap than Chancery flesh and blood could stand. See *Gee* v. *National Trust* [1966] 1 W.L.R. 170.

Secondly, the section makes no mention of enforceability by successors in title *against* the local authority in respect of the authority's obligations under the agreement.

At common law the benefit of a covenant will pass to a successor in title and the restrictions as to negativity and registration do not apply. The covenant must benefit land in which the covenantee holds a legal estate, but the covenantor need not hold any land.[6] There is therefore no difficulty in transmissibility as long as the authority's obligation benefits identifiable land owned by the other party.

Thirdly, section 52 can pass the burden only of negative covenants. The section cannot therefore be used to impose obligations to carry out work, or provide facilities, unless the obligation is to bind only the original covenantor (but see [1976] J.P.L. 216).

The major difficulty of section 52 concerns the question of consideration. Must the authority provide consideration, and if so what consideration can it lawfully offer?

The section uses the term "agreement" which although wider than contract is often used to mean contract. In the absence of specific statutory provision no agreement is enforceable unless it is, a contract and is either made under seal or supported by consideration. It is unlikely that a developer will make a gratuitous promise under seal and so the question of consideration is crucial. Section 52 makes no provision for enforcement, but its incorporation of the *Tulk* v. *Moxhay* doctrine suggests that a contractual relationship between the original parties is contemplated.[7] *Ransom & Luck* v. *Surbiton B.C.* [1949] Ch. 180 is the only case where the general nature of section 52 agreements was discussed. The case turned upon the question whether the authority could offer as consideration an undertaking which restricted the future exercise of its statutory powers. The Court of Appeal held that such consideration was unlawful (see below, p. 133), and thus did not need to determine the general question.

It has been suggested on the basis of this case that section 52 creates a special statutory obligation which does not require consideration (see Grant [1975] J.P.L. 501). This is unconvincing. Strong language is required to displace what is one of English law's most firmly entrenched shibboleths. Secondly the language of Lord Greene M.R. in the *Surbiton* case is consistent only with the proposition that the obligation arises out of contract, although as he said (at p. 195) "it goes *beyond* mere contract in that it gets the characteristics of a restrictive covenant." He also emphasised (at p. 195) that "[section 52] is of very limited application: it merely allows local authorities to enforce restrictions as if they had been entered into for the benefit of an adjoining land-owner." Moreover his Lordship discussed what alternative forms of consideration could be provided in order to persuade landowners to enter into section 52 agreements, accepting that the section would be nugatory if no consideration was available. It is thus reasonably clear that consideration is necessary.

The most obvious and useful form of consideration would consist of an undertaking to grant planning permission, or not to take enforcement proceedings, in exchange for planning gain provided by the developer. In one case (*Beaconsfield D.C.* v. *Gams* (1974) 234 E.G. 749) planning permission was granted for the erection of a bungalow subject to an agreement made under a local statute whereby the developer undertook to demolish a farmhouse on other land which he owned. Cantley J. in an unreserved judgment granted the authority an injunction to prevent the permission being implemented until the farmhouse was demolished. His Lordship treated the developer's failure to perform the agreement as a "calculated and flagrant breach of contract" (see [1975] J.P.L. 704). There are however difficulties in accepting that planning permission can constitute consideration. First, the rule that a public authority cannot fetter its discretion seems to be violated in that the authority is effectively binding itself to grant permission (*Stringer* v. *Minister of Housing* [1970] 1 W.L.R. 1281). In *Ransom & Luck* v. *Surbiton B.C.* (above) the Court of Appeal held that an agreement under which a planning authority purports to tie its hands in respect of the future exercise of its powers is unenforceable (see also *Crittenden (Warren Park)*

Ltd. v. *Surrey C.C.* [1966] 1 W.L.R. 25). The same objection applies to any other promise which an authority might make which restricts its statutory functions, *e.g.* a promise not to interfere with existing rights. Moreover an authority would be acting equally *ultra vires* if it took a proposed agreement into account in deciding upon an application for permission unless the content of the agreement involved only matters which could, in any event, be taken into account. (*e.g. George Wimpey & Co.* v. *Secretary of State for the Environment* [1978] E.G. 470). Similarly permission could not be granted in exchange for an undertaking to do something unreasonable. Statutory powers can no more be extended by agreement than they can be fetted.[8] See (1978) J.P.L. 806.

However, section 52 appears to modify the general principles. Subsection (3) provides that "nothing in this section or in any agreement made thereunder shall be construed as restricting the exercise . . . of any powers . . . so long as those powers are exercised in accordance with the provisions of the development plan."

It may be therefore that a section 52 agreement can at least restrain the authority within the terms of the development plan.

A final limitation of section 52 is that it applies only to agreements to restrict or regulate "the development or use of the land." Thus outright gifts of land are excluded, as are payments of money unless they are "incidental or consequential" to the development or use of the land (section 52 (1)). It is not clear what other positive obligations might fall within section 52, although undertakings to provide facilities or to carry out work on the land itself would certainly do so. But as we have seen positive obligations, cannot under section 52 pass to successors in title.

The third statutory provision deals with this latter difficulty.

Local Acts have in the past conferred powers upon authorities to enter into positive covenants binding upon successors in title (see Jowell [1977] J.P.L. 414, 416). There is also general provision in the Housing Act 1974, 126 (2) (*a*). This provides that an instrument under seal made with a county or district council which contains a "covenant . . . to carry out any works or do any other thing on or in relation to " land shall be enforceable against successors in title to that land.

The drafting of this shows a marked improvement upon section 52. First, it confers liability directly upon successors in title. Secondly, the term "agreement" is not used and any undertaking under seal will therefore be enforceable, even a unilateral undertaking. Thirdly, the section provides its own enforcement machinery, including a provision for the authority to enter the land and carry out the work. This is in addition to any other remedies such as injunction or damages.

However section 126 is limited in scope to covenants involving acts relating to the land itself. It could conceivably include the transfer of land to the authority (which as we have seen is outside section 52, even as regards the original parties). Neither section 126 nor section 52 authorises the payment of money to the authority even in lieu of works carried out on the land. However, as between the original parties the general power in the Local Government Act 1972, s. 111 (above, p. 129) could authorise this.

Finally agreements under both section 52 and section 126 must be registered. The position is affected by the major changes in the law relating to registration brought about by the Local Land Charges Act 1975 (see Law Commission, Transfer of Land; Report on Local Land Charges (1974); Law Com. No. 62). This Act is an attempt to distinguish between public and private obligations binding land. Unfortunately it does not achieve this objective where planning agreements are concerned.

Prima facie any prohibition or restriction on the use of land enforceable by a local authority under any covenant or agreement made with them is a local land charge. (Section 1 (1) (*b*) (ii).) Positive obligations imposed by section 126 of the Housing Act 1974 are also local land charges (1975 Act, s. 1 (1) (*d*); Housing Act 1974, Sched. 1).

If a local land charge is not registered as such it remains binding upon all persons, but a purchaser is entitled to compensation in respect of any loss suffered by virtue of the failure to register (1975 Act, s. 10). By contrast a failure to register an ordinary land charge makes it void against a purchaser (see note [4]). This reflects the public interest in the enforceability of local land charges and it is appropriate therefore that all planning agreements be regarded as local land charges.

However, section 52 agreements seem to be excluded from the company of local land charges. Section 2 of the 1975 Act excludes a number of obligations from the definition, one of these being "a prohibition or restriction enforceable by . . . a local authority under any covenant or agreement being . . . binding on successive owners of the land affected by reason of the fact that [it] is made for the benefit of land of the . . . local authority." This presumably is intended to preserve the principle that ordinary restrictive covenants made with an authority *qua* landowner are registrable in the same way as ordinary land charges.

Section 52 agreements seem to fall within this exemption since their enforceability against successors depends upon the fictitious land owned by the authority. It is doubtful whether Parliament intended that positive and negative planning agreements should thus differ as to enforceability.

However, before the 1975 Act failure to register a local land charge also resulted in the charge being void against a purchaser, and thus the law as to section 52 agreements has not been changed. Nevertheless, the public element in such agreements, particularly in view of the increased use being made of them, suggests that they should no longer be treated merely as restrictive covenants.

The law is bedevilled by unnecessary technicality and the scope of planning agreements is arbitrarily restricted. As is often the case in English law, confusion is caused by a failure to distinguish clearly between public and private law. The policy that informs the private law of restrictive covenants is not appropriate in the context of agreements which seek planning gain.

If planning by agreement is accepted as desirable then a thorough-going revision of section 52 is called for. This should allow positive covenants to run, and also provide for direct enforcement and registration as local land charges. The scope of such agreements ought to be widened, and in particular the circumstances in which the authority's discretion can be restricted should be made clear.

Procedural safeguards too are desirable. These might include provision for publicity and the consideration of objections in respect of some, but not necessarily all, planning agreements.

Notes

1 See Grant [1975] J.P.L. 501; [1978] J.P.L. 8; Loughlin [1978] J.P.L. 290; see also Radcliffe, *Land Policy* (1976), pp. 86–88.

2 *E.g.* lack of "off-site" infra-structure, so that planning permission would otherwise be premature (see Circular 102/72).

3 See also L.G.A. 1972, section 139. Agreements also play a large part in the Community Land Act 1975 scheme. See Grant [1976] J.P.L. 732.

4 See Land Charges Act 1972, s. 4 (6). In the case of registered land restrictive covenants must be protected as minor interests, Land Registration Act 1925, s. 50 (1). See generally Megarry and Wade, *Law of Real Property* (4th. ed.), pp. 753–760.

5 It will also incorporate other aspects of the law of covenants, *e.g.* discharge or modification by the Lands Tribunal (L.P.A. 1925, section 84).

6 The more complex equitable rules for passing benefit are not relevant as long as the original covenantor (*i.e.* the authority) is a party. See also *Smith* v. *River Douglas Catchment Board* [1949] 2 K.B. 500.

7 It has been suggested that "consideration appears to be irrelevant to the enforceability of agreements registered under appropriate legislation" (Grant [1978] J.P.L. 8, 13). Whatever the position is in respect of consideration, the question of registration has no bearing on it. Registration merely gives notice of a covenant (L.P.A. 1925, section 198). It does not affect any question relating to the intrinsic validity of a land charge. Thus if consideration is needed and is missing the charge is unenforceable whether registered or not. Moreover, *Tulk* v. *Moxhay* concerns the question of the transmissibility of an enforceable obligation, and thus presupposes a contract but not necessarily a covenant in the strict sense of a promise under seal. The successor in title whom *Tulk* v. *Moxhay* binds can therefore plead lack of or unlawful consideration.

8 It makes no difference whether or not the authority's intention to make agreements is mentioned in the development plan. Although the development plan is certainly a "material consideration," it cannot in itself extend the range of factors which can legally be taken into account. Moreover, if planning permission is justifiable irrespective of the agreement, then there may be a failure of consideration under the alleged rule excluding the performance of an existing duty (*Morgan* v. *Palmer* (1824) 2 B. & C. 729, where the principle was based upon public policy rather than consideration. *Cf. Collins* v. *Godefroy* (1831) 1 B. & Ad. 950).

Chapter 7

ENFORCEMENT

The law governing the enforcement of development control is
inherently complex and technical. It provoked Harman L.J. to
describe planning as "a subject which stinks in the noses of the
public and not without reason" (*Britt* v. *Bucks C.C.* [1964] 1
Q.B. 77, 87), and more recently was criticised both by the
Divisional Court and the Court of Appeal (*Brooks and Burton*
v. *Secretary of State for the Environment* (1978) 35 P. & C.R.
27, 31 and 47).

The development of the subject since 1947 has been dominated by attempts both by Parliament and by the courts to
reduce the number of cases where enforcement notices have to
be struck down for technical defects. It provides many examples to rebut the common belief that the English judiciary is
excessively sympathetic to private property rights. On the contrary, the cases recognise and make provision for the difficulties
faced by local authorities in taking enforcement proceedings.
Nevertheless a large proportion (about 65 per cent.) of
enforcement notices are challenged, and of these a high proportion (35 per cent.) are successful albeit more frequently on
planning than on legal grounds.[1] One reason for challenging
an enforcement notice is to buy time, since the operation of a
notice is suspended until appeal proceedings are completed, a
process which may run into years (see below, pp. 153–154).

The principal method of enforcement is by service of an

enforcement notice under section 87. This requires the recipient to abate the breach of planning control. Disobedience to an enforcement notice is a criminal offence. Development control can also be enforced by an injunction.

Enforcement Notices

An authority may serve an enforcement notice when "it appears to them" (*sic*) that there has been a breach of planning control after 1963 (section 87 (1)). A breach of planning control consists either of development without permission or of breach of a condition or limitation. There is no obligation to serve a notice, and the decision whether to do so must be taken in the light of "the provisions of the development plan and other material considerations" (*ibid.*). It can thus be challenged in the courts in the same way as a decision upon an application for planning permission. Indeed a citizen could apply for mandamus against an authority which fails to prosecute its functions with sufficient zeal (*cf. R.* v. *Metropolitan Police Commissioner, ex p. Blackburn* [1968] 2 Q.B. 118 and [1973] Q.B. 241). The question of *locus standi* will however be a prime consideration.

A notice is valid even where no breach of planning control has in fact taken place (*Jeary* v. *Chailey R.D.C.* (1973) 26 P. & C.R. 280). This is because it need only "appear to the authority" that there has been a breach and also reflects the general proposition that mistakes of law or fact do not in themselves invalidate government action. Thus it is no defence to maintain that development did not take place unless the authority's belief is totally unreasonable (see below, p. 152 for an exception). It is important to bear in mind that the offence consists of disobedience to an enforcement notice and not breach of planning control as such. The validity of the notice is therefore the central issue.

Errors of law or fact in the notice can however be raised by appealing to the Secretary of State under section 88. This is in general the only way of raising the issue whether or not there has been a breach of planning control (see below, p. 149).

There are important provisions regarding the time limit for serving an enforcement notice. In the case of change of use development the change must, subject to one exception, have taken place after 1963.[2] Changes of use before 1964 occupy a curious limbo, since they are immune from enforcement notice procedures but at the same time cannot be admitted to the company of lawful uses (see above, p. 75).

It may be difficult, particularly in the case of development by intensification, to specify the exact date upon which the change of use took place. Even where the relevant change took place after 1963 the date is still important, because the notice must specify the steps required to remedy the breach of control. It must therefore, in cases of intensification and also in dealing with ancillary uses, preserve the level of activity which existed immediately prior to the alleged change of use (*Mansi* v. *Elstree R.D.C.* (1964) 16 P. & C.R. 153). The correct date is a question of fact for the authority, with which the court will not interfere in the absence of unreasonableness. In cases of "creeping" intensification, for example, it may suffice to preserve the level of activity as it existed on January 1, 1964 (see *Trevors Warehouses* v. *Secretary of State* (1972) 23 P. & C.R. 215; *de Mulder* v. *Secretary of State* [1974] Q.B. 792, 798–799).

A person who seeks the benefit of this time limit can apply for a certificate of established use (section 94). This records the existence of uses which have subsisted continuously since before 1964, either without permission or in breach of a condition, and of uses which started after 1963 but without there being any change of use since 1963 which required planning permission (*Bolivian Tin Trust Co.* v. *Secretary of State* [1972] 1 W.L.R. 1481). The certificate can be issued by the local planning authority upon the application of any person interested in the land, appeal lying as usual to the Secretary of State. The terms of a certificate are conclusive in respect of enforcement notices served after the date of the application for the certificate (*Broxbourne B.C.* v. *Secretary of State* [1979] 2 All E.R. 13).

In the case of operational development and also of change of use *to* use as a single dwelling-house, a time limit applies to the service of an enforcement notice, of four years from the date of the breach (section 87 (3): the certificate of established use machinery does not apply in either case).

This provision raises several problems. First, it seems that where an activity which took place, say, in 1976, constituted both an operation and a material change of use, then enforcement proceedings can be taken against the use but not the operation. It may however be held unreasonable for a notice to be served in such circumstances (*Burn* v. *Secretary of State* (1971) 219 E.G. 586. But see section 87 (7)).

Secondly, the exact moment when the breach takes place may be difficult to establish. In the case of mining operations we have already seen that each "bite with the shovel" is a separate operation (*cf. Thomas David (Porthcawl) Ltd.* v. *Penybont R.D.C.* [1972] 1 W.L.R. 1526). Thus time will never run against mining operations. This analysis probably does not apply to other kinds of operation, so that, for example, the building of a house constitutes a single operation (*Copeland B.C.* v. *Secretary of State*, above, p. 51), the test being whether the operation produces something which is complete in itself, as for example a house or a shovelful of minerals (see (1973) 36 M.L.R. 430). It is thus necessary to decide whether time runs from the beginning or the completion of the operation. The Secretary of State takes the view that "substantial completion" is the test. However, this appears to be based upon the wording of the 1962 Act, which referred to the "carrying out" of the development (section 45 (2) (*a*)). Under the 1971 Act time runs from "the date of the breach" (section 87 (3)). There is no doubt that this is the beginning of the operation, since to hold otherwise would mean that no notice could be served at all until a building had been completed, which is not only absurd but opens the way to wholesale evasions of planning control.

It is also uncertain how the time limit rules apply to breaches of condition. The four-year rule applies to any condition relating to the carrying out of operations. However, it is doubtful whether such conditions can be effectively time-barred. A planning conditions is arguably a continuing obligation, so that a fresh breach takes place on each day during which it is not obeyed. On this view time will never run against such a condition. The Secretary of State, however, holds that time runs from the date the condition was first broken (*cf.* [1967] J.P.L. 189), except where the condition prohibits some seasonal or intermittent activity such as bringing caravans on to land. Here time runs afresh each time the act takes place ([1976] J.P.L. 229).

There is no authority directly in point. However, in *St. Albans District Council* v. *Norman Harper Autosales Ltd.* (1978) 35 P. & C.R. 70, it was held that failure to comply with an enforcement notice by erecting a building which was too large was not a continuing offence and was therefore committed only on the date when it first took place. This provides an analogy in support of the Secretary of State's view.

Service of a notice

An enforcement notice must be served[3] upon the owner and occupier of the land and upon other persons whose interest in the land the local authority considers to be materially affected. The definition of owner is an artificial one, and the "owner" for this purpose is not necessarily the same person as the owner who receives notice of an application for planning permission (see above, p. 79). "Owner" means "a person other than a mortgagee not in possession who . . . is entitled to receive the rack rent of the land or where the land is not let at a rack rent would be so entitled if it were so let" (section 290 (1)). The meaning of this is obscure, and depends upon the application of the law of landlord and tenant to an actual or hypothetical rent. There can, it seems, be more than one owner. Thus a landlord and tenant are both the "owner" where the tenant has sub-let at a rack rent. If however the freeholder lets rent-free or at a low rent the hypothesis of a rack rent cannot, according to one case, apply, so that he is not the owner (see *London Corporation* v. *Cusack-Smith* [1955] A.C. 337). It is difficult to see the relevance of these considerations in the present context.[4]

The definition of "occupier" has been left to the courts, who have eschewed private land law concepts in favour of treating the question as one of fact. An occupier is a person who is in occupation of the land on a permanent basis, whether or not he has an estate in the land. Thus a dweller on a permanent caravan site is an occupier, even though as against the owner he is a mere licensee (*Stevens* v. *Bromley B.C.* [1972] Ch. 400; *Munnich* v. *Godstone R.D.C.* [1966] 1 W.L.R. 427. *cf. Caravans & Automobiles Ltd*. v. *Southall B.C.* [1963] 1 W.L.R. 690; *Courtney-Southan* v. *Crawley U.D.C.* [1967] 2 Q.B. 930).

At one time a notice was void if it was not served on all persons entitled to service. Moreover, all had to be served on the same date, the theory being that an enforcement notice is one, not several notices, and must take effect a prescribed number of days after service (see below, p. 148, *Bambury* v. *Hounslow B.C.* [1966] 2 Q.B. 204, doubted on this point in *Stevens* above).

These defects no longer invalidate the notice. Under the 1971 Act (which re-enacts reforms made in 1968), failure to serve or improper service is a ground of appeal to the Secretary of State, who can disregard these defects if neither the appellant nor the person who was not served has suffered substantial prejudice (section 88 (4) (*b*)).

A problem which has caused considerable concern is that local planning authorities have found it difficult to acquire information about the land and its history on which to base its decision whether to serve a notice. This is one reason why a large proportion of appeals against enforcement notices are successful upon planning grounds.

However, the Town and Country Planning (Amendment) Act 1977 has extended the authority's power to require information, which previously was restricted to matters concerning the identity of persons interested in the land (section 284). The authority is now empowered to require in writing that information be given as to the use of the land and its planning history, it being an offence to withhold such information without reasonable excuse. Moreover, under section 280 (1) the authority can enter land for the purpose of carrying out a survey.

Form and Content of Notice

It is here that the courts' reluctance to strike down notices upon technical grounds is most obvious. There is no compulsory standard form of notice, and authorities are left to draft their own documents, sometimes with disastrous results, judging by the large amount of litigation which enforcement notices attract (see circular 153/74 for a model form of notice).

The Act merely requires that the notice contain certain information. It need not use any particular form of words or technical language. In *Eldon Garages* v. *Kingston-upon-Hull B.C.* [1974] 1 W.L.R. 276, Templeman J. emphasised that rigid statutory recitals were unnecessary and deprecated the use of what he regarded as "magic words" or "ritual incantations." The notice is valid if, read as a whole, and in the light of the recipients' knowledge of the land—but not of other documents (*Miller-Mead* v. *Minister of Housing* [1963] 2 Q.B. 196, 224)—it conveys the required information. This approach, though superficially attractive, is arguably too crude. Technical language is intended to achieve nothing other than precision and certainty. Moreover enforcement notices bind not only their recipient but his successors in title, and it is thus undesirable to rely upon the recipients' knowledge as an aid to construction (*cf. Hawkey* v. *Secretary of State* (1971) 22 P. & C.R. 610. It is difficult to see why formal statutory formulae should not be required.

The Act requires first that the notice state the nature of the breach. This includes a statement of the facts (*East Riding C.C.* v. *Park Estate Bridlington* [1957] A.C. 223), and a description of the kind of breach. This need not consist of a detailed analysis, but must at least state whether the breach consists of development without permission or breach of a condition[5] (*Miller-Mead* v. *Minister of Housing*; *Eldon Garages* v. *Kingston-upon-Hull B.C.*, above). A notice which does this will be valid even if for example it incorrectly describes a change of use, as long as the facts alleged constitute a material change of use (*Brooks and Burton Ltd.* v. *Secretary of State for the Environment* (1978) 35 P. & C.R. 27).

The notice need not identify the relevant planning unit (*Hawkey* v. *Secretary of State*, above). It is enough that it identifies the land where the breach of control is in fact taking place, although it can prohibit development in respect of the whole unit (*Thomas David (Porthcawl) Ltd.* v. *Penybont R.D.C.* [1972] 1 W.L.R. 1526). What it must not do is artificially to restrict the landowner's use rights over his whole unit by arbitrarily dividing up the unit and serving separate enforcement notices in respect of each part. This could have the effect of requiring the same level of use over the whole unit, whereas the developer is prima facie entitled to concentrate his use wherever he wishes within the unit. There would be a heavy onus upon an authority to show a good planning reason for so dividing up the unit (see *de Mulder* v. *Secretary of State* [1974]

Q.B. 792).

Words in an enforcement notice need not be given a strict legal meaning. Thus an enforcement notice was upheld which described a number of derelict lorries as "vehicles," the court refusing to apply the subtleties of road traffic law to the question (*Backer* v. *Uckfield R.D.C.* (1970) 21 P. & C.R. 526; see also Hammersmith L.B.C. v. *Secretary of State* (1975) 30 P. & C.R. 19).

Secondly the notice must specify the steps required to remedy the breach. It must require first that steps be taken to restore the land to its condition before the unauthorised development took place. The authority can probably exercise a discretion to require less than full restoration (*cf. Iddenden* v. *Secretary of State* [1972] 1 W.L.R. 1433; *Copeland B.C.* v. *Secretary of State* (1976) 31 P. & C.R. 403, but in both cases the point was *obiter*). Conversely, the notice must expressly preserve any existing rights (see above, p. 141). Secondly, the notice can require compliance with a condition or limitation.

The powers are somewhat limited. There is no power to require works to be carried out as an alternative to restoration. For example, an unauthorised extension to a building might be acceptable if minor modifications or landscaping were carried out. This can be achieved at present by the Secretary of State granting a conditional planning permission in appeal proceedings against the notice, a procedure both unnecessary and time-consuming. It is likely that many of the issues could be dealt with entirely at local level, either by requiring remedial works or by granting planning permission subject to conditions. At present this cannot be done without an express application for planning permission.

The Secretary of State has accepted in principle recommendations along these lines which were made in the Dobry Report (see Circulars 113/75 and 9/76), but no legislation has so far been introduced.

An enforcement notice cannot issue in respect of development not yet begun or which has ceased. Thus temporary and intermittent activities such as "pop" festivals are effectively beyond the reach of planning controls. There is something to be said for making development without permission a criminal offence *per se*, although it may be argued that the definition of development concerns matters inherently inappropriate to be determined by an ordinary court.

Finally the notice must specify two dates. The first is the date upon which the notice becomes effective. This must be at least 28 days after service during which time an appeal can be made to the Secretary of State. Secondly a time limit must be prescribed for compliance with the notice. This is a matter for the authority's discretion. It is worth noting that the notice does not need to state the penalties for breach or to provide information about rights of challenge. It would be desirable if this information were to be included.

Challenging Enforcement Notices

There are two methods of challenging an enforcement notice. First, if it is *ultra vires* it can be challenged in the ordinary courts upon the basis that it is a nullity and thus totally ineffective ("waste paper," *per* Upjohn L.J. in *Miller-Mead* v. *Minister of Housing* [1963] 2 Q.B. 196, 226). A challenge can be either direct by means of an application for judicial review (see above, p. 107), or collateral, where the citizen exposes the nullity of the notice, for example, by defending a prosecution, or taking proceedings for trespass in respect of any entry on to his land. He can also use force against any official who enters his land in reliance upon an *ultra vires* notice (see *Stroud* v. *Bradbury* [1952] 2 All E.R. 76: "when the [council official] arrived the appellant obstructed him with all the rights of a free-born Englishman and defied him with a clothes prop and a spade"; *per* Lord Goddard C.J., at p. 77). English law offers no general defence to a person who relies upon an invalid governmental act.[6]

Secondly an appeal lies on prescribed grounds to the Secretary of State under section 88, and from him to the court on a point of law (section 246).

It is important to appreciate the general relationship between these remedies. They are in theory entirely distinct. The exercise of a right of appeal which can be conferred only by statute does not depend upon a notice being invalid under the general law. Indeed an appeal presupposes that the decision is valid, since if a decision is void there is nothing to appeal against (*Ridge* v. *Baldwin* [1964] A.C. 40; *Leary* v. *National Union of Vehicle Builders* [1971] Ch. 34; *Stringer* v. *Minister of Housing* [1970] 1 W.L.R. 1281, where the general principle was circumvented in the particular statutory context—1971 Act, s. 36 (3)).

Two consequences follow from this. First, if a notice is *ultra vires* a statutory right of appeal cannot be exercised, and it can be challenged only by way of judicial review (*Chapman* v. *Earl* [1968] 1 W.L.R. 1315; *Stringer* v. *Minister of Housing* (above); *R.* v. *Jones (Gwyn)* [1969] 2 Q.B. 33; *Harman* v. *Official Receiver, Petitioning Creditors & Trustee* [1934] A.C. 244). Thus if a right of appeal is in fact exercised then the appeal decision, whatever its intrinsic merit, is itself a nullity and does not prevent the citizen from later challenging the enforcement notice in the courts (*Ridge* v. *Baldwin*, above; *cf. Swallow & Pearson* v. *Middlesex C.C.*; [1953] 1 W.L.R. 422) see also *Denten* v. *Auckland City Council* [1969] N.Z.L.R. 256, 268–269. Conversely, an authority could, if dissatisfied with the result of an appeal, rely upon the nullity of its own enforcement notice. The Secretary of State can never amend a nullity.

Secondly, if grounds of appeal are prescribed by statute, then *ex hypothesi* matters included in these grounds cannot make the enforcement notice a nullity. A statutory right of appeal must be regarded as the exclusive remedy.

These principles were applied by the Court of Appeal in *Miller-Mead* v. *Minister of Housing* [1963] 2 Q.B. 196 (see pp. 221, 222, 227, 233, 239–240).

Before 1960 there existed only a limited right of appeal against an enforcement notice. This lay to justices and concerned essentially the question whether a breach of control had taken place. Thus mis-recitals and formal defects in the notice, if challengeable at all, had to be brought within the *ultra vires* doctrine. The courts at this time regarded enforcement notices as penal matters and construed them strictly in favour of the individual (see, for example, *East Riding C.C.* v. *Park Estate (Bridlington) Ltd.* [1957] A.C. 223). This made the enforcement of development control a demanding and uncertain activity and there was much criticism of the technicality of the law.

The Caravan Sites and Control of Development Act 1960, in an attempt to alleviate the problem, introduced the present right of appeal to the Secretary of State, who is empowered to correct any informality, defect or error in the notice, if satisfied that it is not material (section 88 (2)). This has been construed generously to mean that any error can be corrected if this can be done without causing injustice in the particular circumstances (*Miller-Mead*, above, at p. 221; *Hammersmith L.B.C.* v. *Secretary of State* (1975) 30 P. & C.R. 19; *Morris* v. *Thurrock B.C.* [1975] J.P.L. 727; *Patel* v. *Betts* (1977) 243 E.G. 1003). Conversely, the Secretary of State must quash a notice which contains a material error.

In the light of this is was held in *Miller-Mead* that mistakes in the notice do not make it invalid, and thus the only method of challenge for mistake is by appeal to the Secretary of State. If the right of appeal is not exercised, then the defect cannot be raised as a defence to prosecution. The statutory appeal provisions assume that the Secretary of State, rather than the court, is the tribunal best qualified to deal with these matters.

A notice is a nullity only if it is defective on its face, in the sense that it is either incomplete or uncertain. If it omits any of the information required by the statute it is void (*cf. Burgess* v. *Jarvis* [1952] 2 Q.B. 41; *Eldon Garages* v. *Kingston-upon-Hull B.C.* [1974] 1 W.L.R. 276), but if the information stated is incorrect, the only remedy is an appeal.

A notice will be void for uncertainty only in an extreme case. The test laid down by Lord Upjohn in *Miller-Mead* [1963] 2 Q.B. 196 at 226-227, 232 has been consistently applied: "Does the notice tell him fairly what he has done wrong and what he must do to remedy it . . .?" (see *Metallic Protectives Ltd.* v. *Secretary of State* [1976] J.P.L. 166). This reflects the broad approach taken by the courts to the construction of enforcement notices.

The grounds of appeal are as follows (section 88 (1)):

(*a*) that planning permission ought to be granted. This is a policy matter and is the ground which most often succeeds.

(*b*) that matters alleged in the notice do not constitute a breach of planning control.

This covers the legal issue whether development has taken place, but it does not seem to provide for an error of fact in the notice where, for example, the allegations which it makes are untrue (*cf. Hammersmith L.B.C.* v. *Secretary of State* (1975) 30 P. & C.R. 19). Since there is no other way of challenging a notice for error of fact, a simple amendment is required.

Grounds (*a*) and (*b*) can be pleaded together. Indeed every appeal is deemed to be an application for planning permission (s. 88 (7)). Conversely an appellant accused of violating the terms of a planning permission is not estopped from arguing that no planning permission is required (*East Barnet U.D.C.* v.

B.T.C. [1962] 2 Q.B. 484), since an unnecessary planning permission is a nullity (but see above, p. 43 n.).

Grounds (*c*) and (*d*) concern the time limit for service of a notice (see above, p. 148).

Ground (*e*) involves defects in the service of the notice (above, p. 143).

Ground (*f*) is that the requirements of the notice are excessive, and ground (*g*) that the period for compliance is unreasonably short. In the last two cases the Secretary of State may vary rather than quash the notice (s. 88 (5)).

These appeal arrangements thus demarcate the spheres of court and Secretary of State.

Unfortunately though the Act has complicated matters by introducing the possibility that the grounds of appeal can sometimes be raised elsewhere. Section 243 (1) provides that "the validity of an enforcement notice shall not except by way of appeal be questioned in any proceedings whatsoever on any of the grounds specified in section 88 (1), (*b*) to (*e*). Furthermore section 243 (2) states that section 243 (1) does not apply to a person who has not been served with the notice and who neither knew nor could reasonably have been expected to know of it. If the view put forward above is accepted, section 243 (1) is superfluous.

Nevertheless, section 243 (1) does not cover grounds (*a*), (*f*) and (*g*), and section 243 (2) clearly presupposes that the appeal grounds can be raised elsewhere, since otherwise the exemption it gives to persons not served would be meaningless.

To give effect to these provisions we thus have to make the bizarre assumption that violation of grounds (*a*). (*f*) and (*g*) affect the validity of the notice, and that the recipient can thus choose between appealing to the Secretary of State, who can amend the notice, or raising the matter as a defence in which case the notice is totally inoperative. The position is most curious where ground (*a*) is concerned, since this is purely a matter of policy, which could not on any view be raised in legal proceedings. Grounds (*f*) and (*g*) could arguably be treated as matters of validity, but even these involve mixed questions of law, fact and policy more appropriate for the Secretary of State than the court. Moreover the court, unlike the Secretary of State, cannot amend the notice but must quash it entirely.

In *Smith* v. *King* (1970) 21 P. & C.R. 560 the Divisional Court held that ground (*g*) could indeed be raised as a defence to prosecution. The majority reached this conclusion with reluctance upon the basis only that section 243 (1) must be taken to mean something! *Smith* has been subsequently followed with equal reluctance (*Hutchinson* v. *Firetto* [1973] J.P.L. 314; *Redbridge B.C.* v. *Perry* (1976) 33 P. & C.R. 176). Lord Parker C.J., dissenting, took the view that grounds (*a*), (*f*) and (*g*) were omitted because they would not affect the validity of the notice anyway and thus there were no other proceedings in which they could be raised. This is consistent with principle but it is unconvincing as an interpretation of the subsection's intention, since none of the grounds of appeal can *ex hypothesi* affect the validity of the notice. Moreover, how does section 243 (2), dealing with persons not served, fit into this? Are we to say that the appeal grounds make a notice void as against these persons but not anyone else? This would be a novel but not unattractive application of the notion of relative nullity (*cf. Durayappah* v. *Fernando* [1967] 2 A.C. 337), to hold that the scope of a statutory power depends upon who is seeking a remedy. A person who has not been served could however best be protected by making failure to serve an express statutory defence along the lines of that provided by the Statutory Instruments Act 1946, s. 4. Section 243 (1) could well be dispensed with entirely.

It has already been noted that appeal proceedings can be used as a delaying tactic since the operation of a notice is suspended until the final determination of an appeal (section 88

(3)). This will cover at least 28 days, which is the minimum period allowed before the notice takes effect, and if an appeal is launched there is added the time taken to decide it, which could be well over a year, as well as the time taken by any subsequent appeal to the court, which could extend into several years if the matter reaches the House of Lords. If no appeal is made to the courts the notice is reactivated 28 days after the Secretary of State's decision, unless he provides for a longer period of grace.[7]

However, the Act provides machinery which in some cases allows acts to be prohibited before the enforcement notice takes effect. Section 90 (as modified by the Town and Country Planning (Amendment) Act 1977) empowers an authority to issue a "stop notice" at any time after serving an enforcement notice but before the latter takes effect. The effect of a stop notice is to prohibit the carrying out of any activity specified in it which is alleged to be a breach of control in the enforcement notice. Stop notices apply to all operational development, which includes for this purpose the deposit of refuse, and to uses which began not more than 12 months before, except use of a building as a dwelling-house or land as a caravan site occupied by any person as his only or main residence.[8] Stop notices are not confined to persons who were served with the enforcement notice (and *cf.* section 90 (6)), but can also be served upon any person who appears to the authority to be engaged in the prohibited activity. The penalty for disobedience is a fine of £400 upon summary conviction, or an unlimited fine on indictment (see below, p. 155), and a further fine of £50 per day (or an unlimited sum on indictment) for continuing the offence. It is a defence to show that the accused neither knew nor could be expected to know of the notice (section 90 (8)).

The stop notice procedure has existed only since 1968, and authorities have made little use of it. One reason for this may be that in certain circumstances they are obliged to pay compensation to the occupier or a person interested in the land. However, this applies only where the enforcement notice or the stop notice is withdrawn or where the enforcement notice is quashed or varied on grounds (b)-(g) of the appeal grounds, which concern essentially legal defects (section 177). Thus if the enforcement notice fails on policy grounds, then no compensation is payable. The compensation provisions do not mention a case where the enforcement notice is held by the court to be a nullity. The position here seems to be that the stop notice is also a nullity, since its validity depends upon the service of an enforcement notice. Thus the recipient should either ignore it or challenge it by an application for judicial review. If he obeys, then it seems that he cannot be compensated (see *O'Connor* v. *Issacs* [1956] 2 Q.B. 288). This well illustrates one of the weaknesses of English administrative law in that the logic of the *ultra vires* doctrine, regarded as a bastion of the rule of law, operates indiscriminately both for and against the citizen.[9]

Compensation is payable only in respect of loss *directly* attributable to the stop notice. This raises difficult problems of causation, but includes in any event money paid in respect of a breach of contract caused by obeying the stop notice (*e.g.* cancelling building work; section 177 (5)).

Penalties for Disobeying a Notice

These are sometimes said to be inadequate (see Dobry, p. 155).

First, there is on summary conviction a fine of up to £400 and upon subsequent conviction £50 per day thereafter. For a large developer this amount is negligible. There is the possibility of an unlimited fine upon indictment, but local authorities are reluctant to entertain the expense and delay of trial by jury.

Proceedings can be taken against the person who was the

owner of the land at the time the notice was served upon him
(section 89 (1)). However, if he subsequently ceased to be
owner his successor in title is liable to conviction and, provided
that he took all reasonable steps to secure compliance, the
original owner has a defence (section 89 (2) and (3); *cf.*
Whitfield v. *Gowling* (1974) 28 P. & C.R. 386).

Where the notice requires the discontinuance of a use or the
compliance with conditions, proceedings can be taken against
any person who either uses the land or causes or permits its use
(section 89 (5)), whether or not such person has been served
with the notice.

These two provisions are mutually exclusive. Thus an owner
out of possession will not be liable for failure to discontinue a
use unless he "causes or permits the use,"[10] and so a landlord
will not be liable for his tenant's user, unless the user is
contemplated by the lease or he is able to take steps to prevent
the use (a covenant against unlawful user) (see *Johnstone & Co.*
v. *Secretary of State* (1974) 28 P. & C.R. 424; *Redbridge L.B.C.*
v. *Perry* (1976) 33 P. & C.R. 176; *Bromsgrove D.C.* v. *Carthy*
(1975) 30 P. & C.R. 34). This, however, does mean that a
landlord may be forced to institute litigation.[11]

In addition to the criminal sanction an authority can enter the
land and take any steps required to remedy the breach, except
the discontinuance of a use. Their expenses are recoverable as a
civil debt from the then owner of the land (section 91 (1)).
However, any expenses the latter incurs, either in respect of
debts to the authority or in obeying the notice himself, can be
recovered from the person who actually committed the breach
of control (*e.g.* occupier or previous owner), for whom the
owner is deemed to incur the expense as agent (section 91 (2)).

An enforcement notice is registrable as a local land charge,
and unless withdrawn or overridden by a later planning
permission (section 92), remains binding permanently upon the
land, thus preventing landowners from buying time by obeying

the notice and then resuming the unlawful development in the belief that fresh proceedings will have to be initiated.

Injunctions

An injunction will lie to restrain a breach of planning control upon the application either of the local planning authority (L.G.A. 1972, section 222) or of the Attorney-General as guardian of the public interest (*Att.-Gen.* v. *Bastow* [1957] 1 Q.B. 514; see above, p. 4). The basis upon which an injunction issues is that the planning legislation creates public rights. It is thus not necessary to show that an offence has been committed. An injunction can issue to restrain development without planning permission, even where no enforcement notice has been served, since it is now clear that development without permission is unlawful *Att.-Gen.* v. *Smith* [1958] 2 Q.B. 173; *LTSS Print & Supply Co. Ltd.* v. *Hackney L.B.C.* [1976] 2 W.L.R. 253).

Unlike an enforcement notice, an injunction can also prohibit breaches of control which are merely anticipated, although the threat must be a strong one (*Att.-Gen.* v. *Morris* (1973) 227 E.G. 991). Injunction proceedings are moreover quicker than enforcement notices and an interim injunction can be obtained in a matter of hours. A mandatory injunction can require the performance of positive acts, *e.g.* compliance with conditions. The injunction also avoids the opportunities for delay provided by the machinery for appealing against enforcement notices. Indeed, if injunction proceedings can be used as a substitute for the enforcement notice, the citizen's position is considerably weakened. First the penalty, which can be unlimited imprisonment for contempt, is more severe. Secondly, he loses the statutory right of appeal to the Secretary of State which, although it may be a delaying tactic, does allow a second hearing on fact and policy, these being matters which the court would be reluctant to investigate.[12]

The injunction is however a discretionary remedy. Thus the court could refuse to intervene on the ground, for example, of delay, hardship, or the lack of damage (*Att.-Gen.* v. *Harris* [1960] 1 Q.B. 31). On the other hand it will also take into account the undesirability of a developer profiting from his unlawful act (*Thanet D.C.* v. *Nidedrive Ltd.* [1978] 1 All E.R. 703).

We have already pointed out the general objection to allowing the statutory machinery to be by-passed in favour of the injunction (above, p. 5).

It is clear, however, that where the Attorney-General is the applicant the court cannot refuse to issue an injunction upon the ground that the statutory enforcement machinery should be used. The Attorney-General's discretion on this point, involving as it does a question of the public interest, has been held to be unreviewable by the court (*Att.-Gen.* v. *Bastow*, above). Nor can the Attorney-General's decision whether to lend his name to relator proceedings be reviewed (*Gouriet* v. *Union of Post Office Workers* [1977] 3 W.L.R. 300), although the basis for this unusual exemption is not clear.[13] It is sometimes claimed that it is justified by the existence of Parliamentary control over the Attorney-General, but this is true of all powers exercised by Ministers, most of which are certainly reviewable. It is also claimed that powers derived from the Royal Prerogative (as this one is) are unreviewable (*cf. Laker Airways* v. *Department of Trade* [1977] Q.B. 643). This, although justified by the authorities (de Smith, *op. cit.*, pp. 253–254), is equally unconvincing in principle.

However, where the authority seeks an injunction in its own name, this statutory power is reviewable and the court may be able to apply the general presumption that the remedy provided by the statute should prima facie be used. However, the court will issue an injunction in cases where the statutory machinery has been used but has proved inadequate (*e.g.*

Att.-Gen. v. *Bastow*, above; *Att.-Gen.* v. *Morris*, above) and other cases where the public interest calls for an additional remedy (*cf. Kent C.C.* v. *Batchelor* (1976) 75 L.G.R. 151: *Stafford B.C.* v. *Elkenford Ltd.* [1977] 1 W.L.R. 324, 329). In either case the onus will be on the authority to justify departing from the statutory procedure. Where an enforcement notice is time-barred, this will be particularly hard to discharge.

The injunction has one major disadvantage over the enforcement notice in that it acts only *in personam*. Thus an injunction can be rendered useless by assigning or leasing the land.

The enforcement procedure would be improved if the relevant sections were redrafted first to be consistent with each other and secondly to dovetail with the general law of judicial review.

Notes

1 See Dobry, pp. 61 and 147–149; also *Development Control Statistics 1977–78* (HMSO).

2 For the significance of this date see Heap, p. 213.

3 For details of method of service see section 283. *Cf. Maltglade Ltd.* v. *St. Albans R.D.C.* [1972] 1 W.L.R. 1230.

4 This definition of "owner" applies (except in sections 27 and 29) throughout the Act "except in so far as the context otherwise requires," section 290 (1). There are few contexts in planning law where such a definition is a natural one and it is suggested that the definition applicable in sections 27 and 29 (above, p. 79) provides a more satisfactory general principle.

5 One difficulty concerns the classification of a breach consisting of a disregard of a time limit attached to a planning permission. This is a breach of condition and not development without permission (*Francis* v. *Yiewsley U.D.C.* [1958] 1 Q.B. 478), except apparently in the case of the 28 days temporary permission granted by the GDO (*Miller-Mead*, above). It seems that a misdescription of this type goes to the substance of the notice and cannot be rectified by the Secretary of State on appeal (see below, p. 150), but see *Garland* v. *Minister of Housing* (1968) 20 P. & C.R. 93, 166. See also *Copeland B.C.* v. *Secretary of State* (1976) 31 P. & C.R. 403.

6 *Cf. Terry* v. *Huntingdon* (1668) Hardres 480; see Sheridan (1951) 14 M.L.R. 270; Akehurst (1968) 31 M.L.R. at 144; there is some authority that enforcement officers are exempt from liability in respect of defects of which they are unaware and which do not appear on the face of the decision documents (*Demer* v. *Cook* (1903) 88 L.T. 629; *O'Connor* v. *Issacs* [1956] 2 Q.B. 288; *cf.* Justices Protection Act 1848, s. 2).

7 Difficulties arise where the Secretary of State improperly refuses to hear an appeal. In *Button* v. *Jenkins* [1975] 3 All E.R. 585 this was held to constitute a "final determination of the appeal," so that the notice became effective when the applicant failed to appeal to the court within 28 days of the Secretary of State's action. This appears to be inconsistent with principle, as it makes the Secretary of State the judge of the limits of his own powers. Normally an improper refusal to determine a matter, where for example it is wrongly believed to be out of time, is treated as *ultra vires* and mandamus will lie. *Cf. R.* v. *Melton and Belvoir JJ.* (1977) 33 P. & C.R. 214, and *Chalgray Ltd.* v. *Secretary of State* (1976) 33 P. & C.R. 10; *Wain* v. *Secretary of State* [1979] J.P.L. 231.

8 See Town and Country Planning (Amendment) Act 1977, s. 1.

9 *Quaere* whether an action for damages in tort may sometimes lie? See Craig (1978) 94 L.Q.R. 428.

10 But they seem to overlap in the case of a failure to comply with a condition, which unlike discontinuance of use, is not excluded from section 89 (1), which imposes liability upon the owner.

11 *Quaere* whether a person can cause or permit a breach of which he is unaware: *Alphacell* v. *Woodward* [1972] A.C. 824; *Impress* v. *Rees* (1971) 69 L.G.R. 305.

12 Strictly speaking the court would in injunction proceedings be entitled to decide on the facts whether there has been a breach of control. All the existing cases involve admitted breaches, but it is unlikely that the court would give less weight to the authority's views on fact or policy than it does in other contexts.

13 *Quaere* also whether delay defeats the Attorney-General (de Smith, p. 392).

Chapter 8

PLANNING APPEALS

An Outline of the Law

There is a right of appeal to the Secretary of State against most development control decisions. We are concerned here with appeals against a refusal or conditional grant of planning permission and against an enforcement notice. The procedure in each case is broadly the same although there are important differences of detail.[1]

The central feature of the procedure is that the appellant and the authority are entitled to a hearing before a person appointed by the Secretary of State (sections 36 (4) and 88 (2)).

In practice this usually takes the form of a local public inquiry presided over by an inspector who is a full-time official employed by the Secretary of State.[2] The procedure is modelled upon that of a court being adversarial and involving legal representatives, speeches, witnesses and cross examination. The inspector also visits the appeal site. After the inquiry the inspector submits a report to the Secretary of State which must contain findings of fact and which usually, but not necessarily, includes recommendations. The Secretary of State is not bound by the inspector's recommendations.

There are some important variations from the normal procedure. First the parties may waive their right to be heard in

161

favour of a shorter and cheaper investigation upon the basis of written representations. This procedure is used in the majority of planning appeals but since the Act entitles them to an oral hearing requires the consent of both parties. Moreover, the Secretary of State is not bound to offer the written representation procedure.[3]

Secondly, in cases prescribed by regulations (see 1971 Act, Sched. 9 and Town and Country Planning (Determination of Appeals by Appointed Persons) Prescribed Classes Regulations 1972 (No. 1652) as amended by S.I.s 1977 Nos. 477 and 1939) the actual decision can be made by the inspector. The Secretary of State does, however, have power to call in any appeal to decide himself.

This procedure is designed to save time in cases involving issues which are only of local concern. It does not raise important questions of principle. Appeal decisions are, in any event, rarely taken by the Secretary of State in person but are delegated to officials. Moreover, in law the inspector's decision is deemed to be that of the Secretary of State so that constitutional propriety is preserved (Sched. 9, art. 2 (3)).

However, the decision taken by the inspector is less likely to be influenced by considerations extraneous to matters discussed at the inquiry. One potential area of conflict is therefore reduced.

Thirdly, the Secretary of State can appoint a planning inquiry commission to inquire into certain planning permission appeals. This consists of between three and five persons and can be used in cases where a special inquiry is necessary either because the appeal involves issues of national or regional importance or because it raises unfamiliar scientific or technical issues (section 48). The commission has two main functions. First, it carries out a general investigation of the case, and secondly, it holds the inquiry instead of the single inspector. It can also institute research projects.

The existence of this machinery provides another statutory indication that planning is intended to have a wide scope.

At the other end of the scale, section 50 empowers the Secretary of State to appoint an independent tribunal to decide planning permission appeals which concern "the design or external appearance of buildings or other similar matters." This sort of issue is unlikely to raise any policy considerations of more than local importance and thus central government involvement, normally a key feature of the planning process, is unnecessary.

Many enforcement notice appeals could equally be entrusted to such a tribunal but neither this nor the commission machinery applies to enforcement appeals. In fact, no use has yet been made of either institution, even though the independent tribunal machinery has been available since 1947.

We must now consider the differences between planning permission and enforcement appeals.

In the former case, the Secretary of State enjoys wider powers. He may decide the appeal as if the application had been made to him in the first instance (section 36 (3)). Thus he is not bound in any sense by the local authority's decision, nor is he denied jurisdiction where the local authority's decision is a nullity (*Stringer* v. *Minister of Housing* [1970] 1 W.L.R. 1281). He is not confined to any stated grounds of appeal and can alter the terms of the permission in any way he wishes.

In the case of enforcement appeals by contrast the Secretary of State's role is more clearly that of an umpire between citizen and authority. The grounds of appeal are prescribed and must be pleaded (*cf. Howard* v. *Secretary of State* [1975] Q.B. 235) and although the Secretary of State can quash the notice, he can vary it only in favour of the appellant.[4] He can moreover grant planning permission for the activities prohibited by the notice.

The judicial character of an enforcement appeal is reflected

H

by the rule that the burden of proof is upon the appellant (*Nelsovil Ltd.* v. *Minister of Housing* [1962] 1 W.L.R. 404).

The position as to burden of proof in planning permission appeals is unsettled. This reflects a basic philosophical uncertainty as to the nature of planning law.

On the one hand it can be argued that an individual has a common law right to do as he chooses upon his land and thus the onus lies with those who seek to refuse permission. Some judicial sympathy was expressed for this view in *Winchester City Council* v. *Secretary of State for the Environment and Jonathan Eccles* [1978] J.P.L. 467. However, we have already seen that the House of Lords refused to recognise a common law presumption in favour of use rights in the context of compensation claims (see above, p. 6). Moreover, as a general principle the onus of proof is on he who asserts. In practice, the Secretary of State's approach is flexible in that he applies a general presumption in favour of granting permission (see Circular 9/76) but may shift the burden of proof according to specific policies (*e.g.* against Green Belt development).

Finally, procedural regulations apply to planning permission inquiries. These take the form of a statutory instrument made by the Lord Chancellor under the Tribunals and Inquiries Act 1971, s. 11 which was a response to complaints that inquiry procedures were not sufficiently fair (see Franks Committee Report, Cmnd. 218 (1957)). These rules embody basic requirements of natural justice and deal *inter alia* with advance notice of the inquiry, the disclosure of information, the publication of the inspector's report, and who is entitled to attend the inquiry (see Town and Country Planning (Inquiries Procedure) Rules 1974 No. 419).[5]

These rules do not apply to enforcement appeals. However their content is largely the same as that of the common law rules of natural justice which do so apply. Thus the law in the two cases differs only where the statutory rules impose procedural requirements additional to those required by the common law. For example, rule 10 entitles the parties to call witnesses and to cross-examine, whereas these rights are not necessarily required by natural justice.

In the case of planning permission appeals, both natural justice and the statutory rules can be invoked. It is however sometimes maintained that where a detailed statutory code of procedure applies this constitutes an exclusive régime and the common law rules do not apply (see above, p. 85). Whatever merits this may have where the procedures are contained in the statute itself, there is no reason why *delegated legislation* should be able to exclude natural justice. The better view is therefore that where the Lord Chancellor's rules fall short of the requirements of natural justice, the latter will prevail.

Problems Relating to the Appeal Machinery— Conceptual Background

The use of the public inquiry with its court-like procedure and its emphasis on the dispute between citizen and authority has attracted considerable criticism upon the theme that legalistic procedures are inappropriate to planning inquiries. These take two main forms. First, it is alleged that the inquiry machinery including its preliminaries and aftermath causes delay, and secondly, that because these are "policy" decisions, undesirable fetters are placed upon the Secretary of State's freedom of action in that an unjustified expectation is raised in the public mind that he who "wins" the inquiry must win the appeal. Discussion of detailed issues of fact and using cross-examination to expose or to reveal administrative errors are described as sterile and regarded as placing an undue burden upon administrators (see E. V. Payne (1971) *Journal of the Royal town Planning Institute* 114; Senior (1961) *Architect's Journal*, June 22).

The use of the term "delay" is question begging. Any decision-making process occupies time but it is legitimate to call it delay only if it is not usefully spent. Thus if the procedure employed is in itself desirable, it cannot be said to cause delay.

The notoriously difficult distinction between "judicial" and "administrative" decisions is also employed in this context in an equally question-begging sense. It is said that planning appeals are administrative in character and that therefore the Secretary of State should be relatively free from procedural fetters (see Franks Committee Report, pp. 262–277).

Three comments must be made upon this. First, the term "judicial" is employed for several different purposes and its meaning varies with the context. In some cases, a decision is judicial if it involves an independent arbitrator settling a pre-existing dispute between two other parties, in others the hallmark of a judicial decision is that it involves the application of rules of law as opposed to policy, and in yet others, any decision is judicial which affects the "rights" of individuals. Sometimes all these elements are cumulatively required (see de Smith, pp. 64–77). As a broad generalisation, the nearer a given procedure is to that of a court of law, the more likely it is to be classified as judicial. In the context of planning appeals, it is the policy element which is said to determine its administrative character.[6]

Secondly, the term "judicial" has meaning only as a conclusion based upon the existence of a given procedure (*e.g.* the presence of procedural trappings). It cannot be used to determine what procedure should be applied to deal with a specific social problem. No issue is inherently judicial. Any area of government activity can be dealt with in broadly two ways, either by framing rules in advance or by entrusting the decision maker with a discretion to make up his own rules. The choice between these broad approaches is one for the legislature and depends upon considerations both of principle and expediency, for example whether the range of fact situations likely to be encountered can conveniently be formulated as definite rules. Prima facie a dispute which can be settled by pre-ordinated rules should be entrusted to an arbitrator independent of the rule-maker, but where the rules to be applied are not fixed in advance, so that the decision-maker has a discretion not only to apply the rules but to create them, then according to our constitutional morality, the decision should be entrusted to an elected body.[7]

However, considerations of expediency may affect this. Some matters may be left to the discretion of a minister because of their political sensitivity or because decisions in individual cases may affect other activities of government. Conversely, a matter may be removed from the "policy" to the "judicial" sphere so that the Government may disclaim responsibility for unpopular decisions.

These considerations explain why planning appeals are decided by the Secretary of State, and involve a large element of discretion.

Thirdly, it is not self-evident that because a decision is based upon policy there should be no procedural fetters upon the decision-maker nor that the traditional techniques of evidence and cross-examination are inappropriate, nor indeed that the decision-maker should not be bound by findings of fact made by someone else.

Planning appeals are not entirely policy decisions but require the Secretary of State to deal with a mixture of law, fact and policy. In many cases, particularly in connection with enforcement appeals, the policy element may be small, hence the power to delegate to inspectors. In the majority it will consist of the application of existing policy to facts and the consideration of how far a given policy should give way to competing considerations, such as other policies or individual hardship, (*e.g.* Green Belt cases). In an exceptional case, the merits of a given policy may be an issue (*e.g.* the Windscale application).

Thus, the sort of policy decision that arises in the case of a planning appeal is not the same as that involved in, say, a structure plan inquiry which involves the formation of policy and not merely its application. The examination in public with its lack of procedural rights and its encouragement of general discussion is appropriate to such an inquiry, but is not a model to be followed in all cases merely by invoking the vague term "policy".[8]

In appeal cases there is a dispute and concrete facts to be determined. What is here meant by "policy" is that the decision-maker has a discretion, although not an absolute one, as to what general rules to apply and the extent to which they should be applied. The essential differences between policy in this sense and law is that the Secretary of State must not bind himself to follow any given policy (see above, p. 101) whereas the reverse is true of a legal rule; and secondly, that he can create as well as apply the rules. There is no necessary difference between the content of a given policy principle and that of a legal rule although in practice, policy principles will often be more imprecise, and refer explicitly to future objectives rather than be couched in language referring to past behaviour.

The traditional techniques of evidence and cross-examination are generally accepted as being the best method of establishing facts. The dispute-orientated adversary procedure has the advantage both of encouraging the participants to leave no stone unturned and to focus attention upon weaknesses in a case. Moreover, if it is accepted that the traditional public inquiry is the best way of discovering facts, then it follows that the Secretary of State should be bound by these facts.

The courts now recognise that the right to be heard is not

dependent on the classification of an activity as judicial.[9] The rules of natural justice apply to administrative as well as to judicial decisions and entitle a party to be heard, for example in connection with a government inquiry into the affairs of a company which satisfies none of the criteria of a judicial decision (*Re Pergamon Press* [1971] Ch. 388).

It must also be remembered that the rules of natural justice are flexible. There are no fixed requirements. Each party has an opportunity to know the other side's case and to put his own, but how this is to be achieved is for the discretion of the inspector in the circumstances of the particular case (see *Local Government Board* v. *Arlidge* [1915] A.C. 120; *Fairmount Investments Ltd. and Southwark Borough Council* v. *Secretary of State* [1976] 1 W.L.R. 1255; *Performance Cars Ltd.* v. *Secretary of State* [1977] J.P.L. 585). The cases contain many judicial warnings against imposing a straitjacket of legal procedures upon those who hold inquiries (*cf. Maxwell* v. *Department of Trade* [1974] Q.B. 523; *John* v. *Rees* [1970] Ch. 345, 398–399). Thus cross-examination is not necessarily required in connection with an enforcement appeal, although there must be a good reason for excluding it (*Miller* v. *Minister of Housing* [1968] 1 W.L.R. 992; *Nicholson* v. *Secretary of State for Energy and National Coal Board* [1978] J.P.L. 39).

Nor does the statute impose any specific procedural requirements although in the case of planning permission appeals, the Lord Chancellor's rules entitle the parties to call witnesses and to cross-examine (*cf.* r. 10 (1)).

The criticisms of the inquiry procedure are directed more against the actual behaviour of the participants, particularly legal representatives, rather than against the law itself. Inspectors tend to give participants considerable latitude, being reluctant to court accusations of unfairness, but a more interventional approach on their part would not be unlawful.

There is room within the existing law therefore to adapt the inquiry procedures to deal with special cases, for example those where wide-ranging examinations of policy are called for, or where alternative sites are proposed (see *Rhodes* v. *Minister of Housing* [1963] 1 W.L.R. 208).

Procedure at the Inquiry

We have already seen that this corresponds broadly to that of a court of law. The detailed provisions of the inquiry procedure rules have been discussed elsewhere (see Hamilton, pp. 200–217). We will concentrate here upon a basic matter of principle, concerning the extent to which the authority must disclose information.

The statutory rules require the authority to disclose at least 28 days in advance all the submissions which it proposes to make at the inquiry and to make available relevant documents. It must be remembered in this connection that any party may claim that the public interest may require that a given piece of information remain secret, the court being the arbitrator of the issue (*D.* v. *N.S.P.C.C.* [1977] 2 W.L.R. 201).

The common law imposes similar requirements in relation to enforcement appeals. Documents must be disclosed sufficiently far in advance to allow for adequate consideration of them, and an adjournment ordered if necessary (*Performance Cars Ltd.* v. *Secretary of State* [1977] J.P.L. 585).

It is uncertain whether the Secretary of State must disclose policy matters. As we have seen, there is no inconsistency between the decision being one of policy and a procedural duty to disclose that policy. Not only is public comment upon policy desirable *per se*, but an appellant can be put to unnecessary expense and inconvenience by instituting an appeal without sufficient awareness of the policy issues involved. It is true that general policy guidance is published and that this is regarded by the inspectorate as authoritative (see *Planning Inquiry*

Practice—J.P.L. Occasional Papers, pp. 3–9). However, matters of emphasis will not necessarily be revealed nor the application of policy to local circumstances, nor such matters as the views of other government departments.[10] Prior to the inquiry, the inspector is furnished with a "regional brief" which is not disclosed to the parties. According to Dobry this merely consists of "a summary of published information of a strategic nature" (p. 130).

The duty to disclose cannot be extended *ad infinitum* to embrace all knowledge in the decision-maker's possession. It is well-established that matters arising out of the tribunal's own experience and expertise need not be disclosed, but these are distinct from "policy" in the sense of general statements of the principles to be applied. It is moreover said that as policy concerns general principle rather than the circumstances of the particular case, a hearing serves no useful purpose (see Wraith and Lamb, pp. 266–277).

This can be answered as follows. First, a duty to disclose policy does not necessarily imply that it can be challenged by evidence and cross-examination in the same way as factual information. Secondly, it seems odd to regard general policy as irrelevant. All rational decisions are an application of general rules to facts. Thus in *Malloch* v. *Aberdeen Corporation* [1971] 1 W.L.R. 1578, the House of Lords held that a schoolteacher who was dismissed for violating regulations was not to be denied a hearing merely because there were no facts in issue and he was obviously in breach. He was entitled to argue that the regulations were invalid. This reasoning applies *a fortiori* to policy rules.

The Franks Committee recommended that policy should be disclosed (pp. 62–63) but this was rejected by the Government.

There is no binding decision on the point, although there are several dicta to the effect that policy need not be disclosed (*Lavender* v. *Minister of Housing* [1970] 1 W.L.R. 1231, 1241;

Summers v. *Minister of Health* [1947] 1 All E.R. 184; *Kent C.C.* v. *Secretary of State* (1976) 33 P. & C.R. 70; *Denton* v. *Auckland City Council* [1969] N.Z.L.R. 263).

However, there are at least two exceptional situations. First, policy which takes the form of a document prepared by an outside body and taken into account by the Secretary of State must be disclosed (*Denton* v. *Auckland C.C.* (above); *French Kier Developments* v. *Secretary of State* [1977] 1 All E.R. 296).

Secondly where a policy is in fact known and relied upon, it cannot be changed without prior notice (*H.T.V.* v. *Price Commission* [1976] 1.C.R. 170; *R.* v. *Liverpool Corporation* [1972] 2 Q.B. 299; *cf. Niarchos (London) Ltd.* v. *Secretary of State for the Environment and Westminster (City) London Borough Council* (1978) 35 P. & C.R. 259, 264).

The rules of natural justice apply also to the written representation procedure. Each party's statement is sent to the other party who has 14 days to comment. Natural justice would probably require that the parties be given further opportunity to answer each others comments, albeit in *Wiseman* v. *Borneman* [1971] A.C. 297 the House of Lords, mindful of the administrative consequences of a continuous exchange of documents, refused to allow an applicant more than one right of reply. *Wiseman* however concerned a preliminary decision in a tax matter where an oral hearing was subsequently held. In the case of a planning appeal by written representations, there is no subsequent oral hearing unless the parties abandon the written procedure in favour of an inquiry. This they can do at any stage.

The Secretary of State's Decision

The traditional doctrine that the Secretary of State is not bound by the findings and recommendations of the public inquiry has been considerably modified both by statute and the courts.

The law is approaching a position where first there is a

presumption in favour of the findings of the inquiry, at least in relation to matters of fact, and secondly the Secretary of State's decision must be rationally justified.

In the first place, the decision must not be based upon any issues or facts which were not raised at the inquiry. This is a rule of natural justice and thus applies to all planning appeals (*Fairmount Investments and Southwark London Borough Council* v. *Secretary of State* [1976] 1 W.L.R. 1255). It applies to new issues raised both by the Secretary of State himself and in the inspector's report. In the *Fairmount* case, the decision was quashed because the Secretary of State took into account evidence that the structure of a house was unstable, which the inspector discovered on his post-inquiry site visit. There is thus a pitfall for the zealous inspector (see also *Hibernian Property Co.* v. *Secretary of State* (1973) 27 P. & C.R. 197; *Sabey* v. *Secretary of State* [1978] 1 All E.R. 586).

This has been embodied in the statutory inquiry procedure rules. By rule 12, where the Secretary of State differs from the inspector on a finding of fact, or takes into account fresh evidence or any new issue of fact, and, as a result, disagrees with any of the inspector's recommendations, he must inform the parties (see below, p. 177) and give them the opportunity to make further representations. In the case of new issues of fact, he must re-open the inquiry if requested. Similar rules apply to inspectors' decisions, except that the question of disagreement does not arise (S.I. 1974 No. 420, r.14).

The duty to disclose under the regulations applies only where the Secretary of State disagrees with an inspector's recommendation. Thus it does not apply where the inspector makes no recommendations. However, the common law may fill this loophole requiring, as it does, disclosure in all cases where there is a risk that the evidence might be material (*Performance Cars Ltd.* v. *Secretary of State* [1977] J.P.L. 585).[11] The rules expressly exempt the Secretary of State from disclosing matters of government policy, but as we have seen, this may sometimes be contrary to natural justice. However, policy as such must be distinguished from "matters of opinion," which both the statutory rules and natural justice agree need not be disclosed since it is here where the essential discretion of the Secretary of State lies. Matters of opinion are value judgments as to how the facts relate to policy, for example, is a proposed building an exceptional case (*Luke* v. *Minister of Housing* [1968] 1 Q.B. 172; *Winchester City Council* v. *Secretary of State for the Environment and Jonathan Eccles* [1978] J.P.L. 467; *Webb* v. *Secretary of State* (1972) 224 E.G. 869); aesthetic judgments (*Vale Estates (Acton) Ltd.* v. *Secretary of State* (1970) 69 L.G.R. 543) or the seriousness of the impact of a proposal upon the locality (*J. Sainsbury & Co.* v. *Secretary of State for the Environment and Colchester Borough Council* [1978] J.P.L. 379). This is an application of the principle referred to above, that judgments based upon the knowledge and expertise of the decision-maker need not be disclosed. However, where a value judgment is based upon external expert evidence, such as a surveyor's report, it must, it seems, be treated as a question of fact (*cf. Coleen Properties* v. *Minister of Housing* [1971] 1 W.L.R. 433—whether acquisition of a building was "reasonably necessary" (see also *Pyrford Properties Ltd.* v. *Secretary of State* [1977] J.P.L. 724; *Camden B.C.* v. *Secretary of State for the Environment + E.M.I. Ltd. + E.M.I. Cinema Properties Ltd.* [1975] J.P.L. 661).

The second restriction upon the Secretary of State's freedom derives from his statutory duty to give reasons in writing for his decisions if requested by the parties (Tribunals and Inquiries Act 1971, s. 12). This applies to all planning appeals and has been construed by the court as requiring that the decision be in effect rationally justified, and correct on matters of fact, a degree of control more detailed than in any other area of judicial review. The statement of reasons must explain what matters influenced the decision and the reason for any disagreement with the inspector, even, it seems, as to matters of opinion (*cf. French Kier Ltd.* v. *Secretary of State* [1977] 1 All E.R. 296). The decision will be quashed if the reasons fail to deal with relevant issues or if the language is obscure or errors are disclosed (*Hope* v. *Secretary of State for the Environment* (1975) 31 P. & C.R. 120; *Ellis* v. *Secretary of State* (1974) 31 P. & C.R. 130). The court will also quash a decision unsupported by evidence (*Niarchos (London) Ltd.* v. *Secretary of State for the Environment and Westminster (City) London Borough Council (1978) 35 P. & C.R. 259; Preston B.C.* v. *Secretary of State* [1978] J.P.L. 548), and one where a change of policy is not explained (*D.F.P. (Midlands) Ltd.* v. *Secretary of State for the Environment* [1978] J.P.L. 319).

The decision letter which contains the reasons can thus be examined in the light of the inspector's report to determine whether the two are consistent. Under the statutory rules, the inspector's report must be disclosed (r. 13 (2)) but it has been held that the common law does not so require *Local Government Board* v. *Arlidge* [1915] A.C. 120; for arguments for and against disclosure, see Franks Committee Report, Chap. 23).

It appears, therefore, that the report need not be disclosed in enforcement cases. In practice, however, the inspector's report is always disclosed, a copy accompanying the decision letter.

In many cases, the Secretary of State's reasons merely consist of a statement that he agrees with the inspector's recommendations and conclusions. In such a case, the inspector's report will be treated as the statement of reasons and examined accordingly (see *Givaudan* v. *Minister of Housing* [1967] 1 W.L.R. 250).

The courts take into account considerations of administrative convenience and, mindful of allegations of excessive legalism and delay, have repeatedly emphasised that decision letters will be construed broadly and not in the manner of statutes or conveyances. Thus the letter need not set out every fact or every issue in the appeal but can confine itself to what the Secretary of State regards as the important issues (*Boyer* v. *Minister of Housing* (1968) 20 P. & C.R. 176); *Vale Estates (Acton) Ltd.* v. *Secretary of State* (1971) 69 L.G.R. 543, 547; *J. Sainsbury* v. *Secretary of State for the Environment and Colchester Borough Council* [1978] J.P.L. 379). However, if it is alleged that a relevant factor has been omitted, the court will quash the decision unless it can be shown that this factor was on balance of probabilities taken into account (*Myton* v. *Minister of Housing* (1963) 16 P. & C.R. 240; see also *Iveagh* v. *Minister of Housing* [1964] 1 Q.B. 395, 410).

It has sometimes been asserted that the court cannot look at the evidence to decide what matters should be included in the report since this would be a usurpation of the inspector's discretion (*Ashbridge Investments* v. *Minister of Housing* [1965] 1 W.L.R. 1320; *Boyer* v. *Minister of Housing* (1968) 20 P. & C.R. 176). However, recent cases seem to negate this. It has been held that the evidence can be admitted not only to establish that a relevant factor has not been taken into account, but also to show "that a particular matter of importance had been completely misunderstood or put in an entirely wrong or misleading way so that the Secretary of State never had the real picture": *East Hampshire D.C.* v. *Secretary of State for the Environment and C. H. Joseph* [1978] J.P.L. 182—which concerned an error of fact. See also *Preston B.C.* v. *Secretary of State* [1978] J.P.L. 548; *Ostreicher* v. *Secretary of State* [1978] 1 W.L.R. 810, 187; *Wimpey* v. *Secretary of State* (1979) 250 E.G. 241.

Participation

The law concerning who is entitled to appear at the inquiry has an element of arbitraryness being governed more by expediency than principle.

We have seen that subject to specific exceptions there is no right to be heard in connection with applications for planning permission (above, pp. 81–85). This is reflected at the appeal stage. The only persons entitled to appear at the inquiry are the appellant, the local planning authority, other local authorities and section 29 parties, who comprise persons who were entitled to make representations in relation to the original application (see rule 7 of the Lord Chancellor's rules). However, any other person may appear at the discretion of the inspector.

This restrictive position has been defended by the Government upon the basis first, that it is impracticable to cater more generously for third parties, and secondly, and somewhat inconsistently, that the position of third parties would not be improved by reforms since in practice, inspectors exercise their discretion generously to admit anyone who wishes to appear (see Wraith and Lamb, pp. 253–263).

However the position of third parties who are allowed to attend is not as good as those who appear as of right. They are not entitled to advance notice of the local authority's case nor to receive documents. They may not call evidence or cross-examine, nor do they enjoy the post-inquiry safeguards such as the right to be informed of disagreements and fresh evidence (above, p. 173).

Added to this, it must be remembered first that there is no right of appeal against an unconditional grant of planning permission, even though it is this to which a third party, such as a local resident, is most likely to object. Moreover, even against a refusal or a conditional grant, only the appellant may appeal.

Thus, where no inquiry is held, only the appellant and the local planning authority have a right to be heard (see above, p. 161). In the case of enforcement notices, the right of appeal is conferred upon anyone upon whom the notice was served, but again only the appellant and the authority have a right to be heard.

These restrictive rules reflect the view that planning legislation is intended to protect the public interest in general and not to confer rights upon particular members of the public (*Buxton* v. *Minister of Housing* [1961] 1 Q.B. 278). It has been held that the public interest includes the interests of individuals such as local residents, but although these must be taken into account, this does not confer *locus standi* upon such individuals (*Stringer* v. *Minister of Housing* [1970] 1 W.L.R. 1281).

The theoretical basis of this is questionable. First, it is difficult to distinguish the abstract notion of public interest from the interests of individual members of the public. Secondly, the proposition that the planning legislation does not confer substantive rights upon individuals (see pp. 3–6, above) does not necessarily mean that they should not have procedural rights.

The present position where third parties are permitted to appear and then treated as poor relations by being denied the full package of procedural rights represents the worst of both worlds and can be justified upon the basis only of administrative convenience. There is a case at least for recognising that organised bodies such as amenity groups should have formal recognition and be consulted in much the same way that many statutes require consultation with interested parties before delegated legislation is made.

It is sometimes argued that lawyers are too concerned with protecting private property rights and fail to recognise that planning is concerned with a wider range of interests than those of the landowners (see McAuslan [1971] P.L. 247). The rules governing attendance at the inquiry are a prime illustration of this. They can be compared with equally restrictive rules governing *locus standi* to challenge the Secretary of State's decision in the courts, but contrasted with the more generous approach taken in certiorari cases (see pp. 180–181, below and p. 32, above).

The lack of a general philosophy both of planning and of judicial review is nowhere more apparent than in connection with *locus standi*.

Challenge in the Courts

The ordinary methods of judicial review do not apply to planning appeals.

The Act provides machinery for challenging planning permission appeals in the High Court and provides that such decisions shall otherwise "not be questioned in any legal proceedings whatsoever" (sections 242 (1) (*e*) and 242 (2) (*a*) and (*b*)). There is authority that clauses which purport to exclude judicial review do not as a matter of construction cover *ultra vires* decisions which being void are not "decisions" at all and therefore not caught by the clause (*Anisminic* v. *Foreign Compensation Commission* [1969] 2 A.C. 147). However, this is merely a presumption of statutory interpretation created by the courts' reluctance to accept restrictions upon their jurisdiction and the position depends entirely upon the specific statutory provision in question. The clause with which we are concerned is found in the majority of statutes concerning land use decisions and has been consistently held to exclude judicial review except by way of the statutory procedure (*Smith* v. *East Elloe R.D.C.* [1956] A.C. 736; *Routh* v. *Reading Corporation* (1971) 217 E.G. 1337; *Hamilton* v. *Secretary of State for Scotland* 1972 S.L.T. 233; *ex p. Ostler* [1977] Q.B. 122 and see (1975) 38 M.L.R. 274, (1978) 41 M.L.R. 383).

The statutory procedure allows challenge within six weeks and thus deserves more sympathetic treatment than provisions which purport to exclude judicial review entirely. Moreover, it is reasonable to believe that land use disputes should be settled quickly. Injustice may arise in cases, for example, of fraud where the defect may not be discovered until after the expiry of the time limit, but an action for damages probably lies in respect of fraudulent misuse of governmental powers.[12] This does not necessitate denying the validity of the decision itself and is therefore unaffected by the clause.

However, in *R.* v. *Secretary of State, ex p. Ostler* [1977] Q.B. 122, the Court of Appeal thought that a decision vitiated by fraud or breach of natural justice, could not be challenged except under the six weeks procedure, but Lord Denning M.R. thought that the position might be different where want of jurisdiction was alleged in the sense of failure to comply with an express statutory requirement.[13] This seems entirely unsatisfactory since this kind of defect is likely to be immediately apparent so that there is no reason why challenge should not be required within six weeks. It is cases of concealed defects such as bad faith where injustice may lie.

The statutory six weeks procedure for challenge is more restrictive than the ordinary judicial review procedure in that *locus standi* is limited to "persons aggrieved." This has been held to include only persons who have a right to appear at the inquiry (*Buxton* v. *Minister of Housing* [1961] 1 Q.B. 278), and other persons where legal rights have been infringed by the decision in question. This second category appears to add little to the first since upon the assumption that the planning legislation in itself confers no rights upon third parties, the only persons whose rights are affected by a refusal of planning permission as such are those with an interest in the land in question. Thus if planning permission is granted for operations which create a nuisance, it is not the permission which causes the nuisance. A planning permission merely removes the ban on development imposed by the Act. The person who carries out the operation is in law the creator of the nuisance. However, the *Buxton* principle has subsequently been extended to give *locus standi* to persons who actually appeared at the inquiry, even though their appearance was by grace of the inspector and not of right (*Turner* v. *Secretary of State* (1973) 28 P. & C.R. 123; *Bizony* v. *Secretary of State* [1976] J.P.L. 306). This reflects the view expressed by Lord Denning that the *locus standi* requirement should be a generous one designed to let in all but the busybody (*cf. Maurice* v. *L.C.C.* [1964] 2 Q.B. 362; see also P.C.A. Annual Report for 1977, p. 30 (H.C. 156)).

The grounds of challenge under the statutory formula are divided into two categories (see section 245 (1)). The first one is that the decision "is not within the powers of the Act." Despite dicta from the House of Lords that this embraces only violations of express statutory requirements (see *Smith* v. *East Elloe R.D.C.* [1956] A.C. 736), it is now settled that it includes all defects which would make the decision *ultra vires* under the general law, such as breach of natural justice and bad faith (*Webb* v. *Minister of Housing* [1964] 1 W.L.R. 1295; *Fairmount Investments and Southwark Borough Council* v. *Secretary of State* [1976] 1 W.L.R. 1255; *Hibernian Property Co.* v. *Secretary of State* (1973) 27 P. & C.R. 197). The second category consists of a failure to comply with "relevant requirements." This includes any error of law or procedural defect (*Gordondale Investments Ltd.* v. *Secretary of State* (1972) 23 P. & C.R. 334; see also (1975) 38 M.L.R. at pp. 280–284).

Thus the six weeks procedure is in one respect wider than the general law of judicial review since the error of law does not have to be on the face of the record. Moreover, a "relevant requirement" includes a requirement not only of the statute but also of any statutory instrument such as the Inquiries Procedure Rules.

There is an overlap between the two categories in that *ultra vires* decisions will *ipso facto* constitute a failure to comply with a requirement, and as we have seen, a breach of the Inquiries Procedure Rules will normally, but not necessarily, constitute a breach of natural justice. However, it seems that disregard of the Inquiries Procedure Rules as such does not make the decision *ultra vires* (*Davies* v. *Secretary of State for Wales* [1977] J.P.L. 102), nor does a failure to give adequate reasons (*Brayhead (Ascot) Ltd.* v. *Berks C.C.* [1964] 2 Q.B. 303; *French Kier Ltd.* v. *Secretary of State* [1977] 1 All E.R. 296).

The difference between the two categories is that under the second head the court may quash the decision only if the interests of the applicant have been "substantially prejudiced" by the failure in question. In cases of *ultra vires* where the public interest is paramount, it may always quash. It has been held, however, that substantial prejudice exists whenever the applicant is denied some benefit to which the Act or the Rules entitle him (*cf. Wilson* v. *Secretary of State* [1973] 1 W.L.R. 1083). Thus a failure to give reasons should entitle the court to quash the decision without requiring further evidence of prejudice.

Under the second head, moreover, the court has a discretion whether to quash the decision since the defects involved would not necessarily affect its validity under the general law. In *Miller* v. *Weymouth and Melcombe Regis Corp.* (1974) 27 P. & C.R. 468, Kerr J. refused to quash a local authority order upon the grounds that the appellant had suffered no prejudice (the defect was an error concerning dates). His Lordship held that the notice was not *ultra vires* but added that the same discretion exists even in the case of an *ultra vires* order. Logical objections to this based upon the notion of nullity are not conclusive. The law does not have to be logical and there are cases where a remedy has been refused even though the decision was *ultra vires* (*e.g. Gregory* v. *Camden B.C.* [1966] 1 W.L.R. 899). The substantive law and that of procedure must be kept distinct. However, under the general law, a decision is still void even where a discretionary remedy is refused and it can thus be challenged by other methods, if for example its validity is relevant to an action in contract or tort (*R.* v. *Williams* [1914] 1

K.B. 608). But in the case of planning appeals, all other methods of attach are excluded and Kerr J.'s approach may thus be too restrictive. In any event *Gordondale Investments Ltd.* v. *Secretary of State* (1971) 23 P. & C.R. 344 provides Court of Appeal authority to the contrary.

The right to challenge under section 245 is not an appeal. The court's power is limited to quashing the decision and it cannot remit the matter to the Secretary of State with directions as to how he should decide it. Such a power to remit does now exist under the general law of judicial review[14] and its absence here is an anomaly.

Enforcement appeals are governed by different provisions. There is a right of appeal to the Divisional Court upon a point of law (section 246 (1)). This must be exercised within 28 days. The court's powers here are wider than in the case of planning permission appeals in that rules of court can be made empowering the court to remit the matter to the Secretary of State with directions. (R.S.C., Ords. 55, 94 (S.I. 1965 No. 1776).)

It must be remembered that this statutory machinery applies only to the Secretary of State's decisions. Where an enforcement notice is void, the general law of judicial review provides the only remedy (above, pp. 148 *et seq.*).

The procedure for challenging appeal decisions is excessively complex. Dobry recommended that the powers of the court be extended to allow review of a decision which is "ambiguous or unreasonable in a comprehensive sense." It is difficult to see what this means. If it is accepted that courts should not be allowed to determine the merits of policy decisions, then the existing law governing the grounds of review goes far enough, bearing in mind what is required in connection with the duty to give reasons (see above, pp. 174–176).

It is the procedural aspects of judicial review which require reform. Now that the general law relating to remedies has been

improved (see above, pp. 108–110), there seems little justification for retaining special statutory machinery for challenge and
in particular for providing different procedures for planning
permission appeals and enforcement notices. The matter is
further complicated because first instance decisions are reviewable under the general law.

It is suggested that the special statutory machinery be
abolished. Matters of delay and *locus standi* are adequately
provided for under the general law of judicial review,[15]
although it may be that a case can be made for retaining a fixed
time limit in respect of planning decisions.

The general law of judicial review also has the advantage that
leave to apply is needed *ex parte* from the Divisional Court, thus
obviating the need at this stage for the department to be
represented.

Notes

1 The same procedure is used for applications "called in" by the Secretary of
State. For public inquiries generally, see Wade, Chap. 24, and Wraith and
Lamb, particularly Chaps. 4, 7, 8.

2 There has been controversy over whether the inspector should be
independently controlled, *e.g.* by the Lord Chancellor. For arguments see
Franks Committee Report, Chap. 21. Since the inspectorate is *de facto*
independent from the policy-making branch of the department, there is much to
be said for strengthening public confidence in the inquiry process by making it
formally independent.

3 See Wraith and Lamb, esp. pp. 198–200. In 1975–76, 71·4 per cent. of
appeals were dealt with by written representations and 75.4 per cent. of appeals
were decided by inspectors (see below) (see *Development Control Statistics
1975–76* (HMSO). Time taken is about 40 per cent. less than by inquiry.
However, written representation procedure is used for simpler cases which
would probably be decided quicker anyway. Moreover, costs cannot be
awarded against a party except in connection with an inquiry. Even here, costs
are only sparingly awarded, *i.e.* against persons guilty of unreasonable
behaviour. See Local Government Act 1933, s. 290 (5); *R.* v. *Secretary of State
for the Environment and Another*, *ex p. Reinisch* (1971) 22 P. & C.R. 102;
Franks Committee Report, Cmnd. 218 (1957) paras. 321–323; Report of
Council on Tribunals, Cmnd. 2471 (1964), Circular 73/65; Dobry, pp.
134–135.

4 Section 88 (5). This must not be confused with the power under section 88 (4) (*a*) to *correct* a defective notice which can be either for or against the appellant.

5 Similar rules apply to inspectors' decisions (see S.I. 1974 No. 420) and to various other land use procedures such as compulsory purchase orders.

6 Policy decisions which involve an inquiry are sometimes called quasi-judicial, see *Johnson & Co.* v. *Ministry of Health* [1947] 2 All E.R. 395.

7 We are not here concerned with realist and other arguments about the extent to which the courts apply policy or create law. Clearly the distinction between rules and policy is one of degree. Even a nominally unfettered discretion is restricted by rules (see Chap. 4 above) but a court's policy discretion is circumscribed to a far greater extent (*cf.* Hart, *The Concept of Law*, Chap. 7).

8 The term "policy" is used in several different senses, some of which, for example "general principle," are too wide to be useful here; *cf.* Marshall, *Justiciability* (Oxford Essays in Jurisprudence), particularly pp. 280–287.

9 Early cases involving public inquiries which depend upon classification of the procedure as "judicial" are still cited in planning law texts, *e.g.* Hamilton, pp. 218–224. These must now be treated with caution although they are still authoritative in that a judicial decision will normally attract natural justice whereas an administrative one may do, and if it does, the detailed requirements of natural justice may be less stringent, *cf. Re H.K.* [1967] 2 Q.B. 617; *Oistreicher* v. *Secretary of State* [1978] 1 W.L.R. 810.

10 The local planning authority will have disclosed its policy before the inquiry because of its duty to give reasons for its refusal or conditional grant of permission. Moreover, the Lord Chancellor's rules require the attendance of representatives of government departments who have expressed in writing views adverse to the appellant. Rule 8 exempts them from being questioned as to the merits of Government policy.

11 There is some authority for the proposition that natural justice requires disclosure only of material which in fact influences the decision adversely to the applicant. See *Lake District Planning Board* v. *Secretary of State* [1975] J.P.L. 220. This seems contrary to the rationale of natural justice which requires that justice appear to be done; *cf. John* v. *Rees and Others* [1970] Ch. 345, 402.

12 See Gould (1972) 5 N.Z.U.L.R. 105; *David* v. *Adbul Cader* [1963] 1 W.L.R. 834. As regards more general liability in tort see *Anns* v. *Merton L.B.C.* [1977] 2 W.L.R. 1024; Law Commission, *Remedies in Administrative Law*, Working Paper No. 40, paras. 147–148.

13 His reasoning presupposed that breach of natural justice and fraud do not make the decision void. This is difficult to reconcile with principle or authority, but see Denning, *The Discipline of Law*, p. 108.

14 R.S.C., Ord. 53 (as amended) (S.I. 1977 No. 1955), r. 9 (4).

15 *Ibid.*, rr. 3 (5) and 4.

Appendix

DEVELOPMENT BY PUBLIC AUTHORITIES

In view of the large amount of land owned by various public authorities (approximately 18 per cent. of the surface of England, Scotland and Wales; see Dowrick [1975] P.L. 10) and of the significant environmental effects of development by public authorities, it is worth outlining the various privileges which these bodies enjoy in relation to development control. It has been suggested that these are excessive (see McLoughlin, *Control and Urban Planning*, p. 51).

A. *The Crown (including land owned by government departments)*

Exempt by section 266 from all development control except where Crown land is developed by other persons having an interest in the land (see Dobry, App. 1). In practice LPAs are consulted in respect of development proposals (see Circulars 80/71 and 7/77).

B. *Statutory undertakers*

These comprise persons authorised by statute to carry on transport undertakings (but not air transport) or to supply electricity, gas, hydraulic power or water: section 290 (1).

(i) Certain repair and maintenance work is not development: section 22 (2) (c).

186

(ii) Much development upon "operational land" (see below) has GDO permission: see GDO 1977, Class XVIII (S.I. 1977 No. 289). This does not normally include the construction or reconstruction of buildings so as to affect design or external appearance, or of plant over 15 metres high. There is also permission for underground pipes, cables etc., but not overhead pylons.

(iii) Development which requires the consent of a government department (section 40), *e.g.* overhead pylons. Here the department in question can direct that permission be deemed to be granted (see *e.g.* Circular 34/76). This includes development where a compulsory purchase order is involved which requires ministerial confirmation (see Drapkin [1974] P.L. 220).

(iv) Other development requires planning permission, but there are procedural privileges in relation to development over operational land (section 224), in that appeals and called-in applications are decided jointly by the Secretary of State and the appropriate Minister (section 225). This does not apply to advertisements (section 241).

(v) There are also special privileges relating to compensation (sections 237–240).

Operational land means land which is either already used for the purpose of the undertaking or which is held with a view to using it in the future, but not land "which in respect of its nature and situation is comparable . . . with land in general" (section 222). This is a question of fact. The land in question need not be contiguous to other operational land: *R.* v. *Minister of Fuel and Power* [1957] 1 W.L.R. 861.

The effect of this seems to be that land used in the same way as it might be used by persons other than statutory undertakers, *e.g.* a stationmaster's house or a showroom or office, is not operational land.

Land acquired before December 6, 1968 (when the Town and Country Planning Act 1968 came into force) is only operational land if

(i) it was operational land under the earlier law; or

(ii) it had planning permission for the purposes of the undertaking or in certain other special circumstances (see section 223).

C. *Local authorities (some will also be Statutory Undertakers, B above)*

(i) Section 40 applies: see B (iii) above.

(ii) Highway Repair and maintenance is not development: section 22 (2) (*b*).

(iii) Certain minor operations have GDO permission (Class XIII and XIV).

(iv) Section 270: local planning authorities can in effect grant themselves permission in respect of development on land owned by them. See Town and Country Planning General Regulations 1976 (S.I. 1976 No. 1419). If they make appropriate resolutions, planning permission is deemed to be granted by the Secretary of State. They must however comply with notice and publicity provisions similar to those imposed in respect of other applications for planning permission (above, pp. 79–82), and comply with directions issued by the Secretary of State, who can call in any proposal for determination by himself.

The "county matter" machinery (above, p. 19) is not applicable, but where a proposal departs from the structure plan the Secretary of State must be notified. He may thus call in the proposal. (This also applies to departures from local plans modified by the Secretary of State.)

Where the proposal involves the alteration or extension of a listed building, application for permission must be made to the Secretary of State.

These requirements can be enforced by means of an injunction (with the aid of the Attorney-General), but subject to that there is little external control.

D. *Other public bodies*

These are subject to ordinary controls, except:

1. *British Airports Authority*. GDO permission for operational land development. This does not include the construction or extension of runways: *ibid*., Class XVIII, H.

2. *Post Office*. GDO permission for operational land development except buildings or machinery exceeding 15 metres in height: *ibid*., Class XVIII,I.

3. *National Coal Board*. (a) GDO permission for development in connection with existing mines. Prior consent of LPA required in the case of buildings, which can be refused on amenity grounds: *ibid*., Class XX.

(b) Opencast mining: procedure analogous to section 40 applies (Opencast Coal Act 1958).

Other mining undertakers have GDO permission for operations in connection with existing mines: see *English Clays* v. *Plymouth Corporation* [1973] 1 W.L.R. 1346; see Telling, pp. 254–258.

(c) The National Coal Board may be treated as a statutory undertaker for certain purposes: section 273.

4. *Sewage authorities*. GDO permission in relation to underground sewers: *ibid*., Class XVI.

5. Other development authorised by statute or by order approved by both Houses of Parliament also has GDO permission subject to the consent of the local planning authority in certain cases: *ibid*., Class XII.

INDEX

191